PRAISE FOR
MESSAGES FROM THE BLACK RECLINER

"An inspirational memoir of how a debilitating illness can be the doorway to a deeper healing than ever imagined. It is a story of healing trauma—traumatic loss, medical trauma, and childhood trauma. A courageous journey of breaking through constraints to build a life that is whole and free."
—Jasmin Lee Cori, author of *Healing from Trauma: A Survivor's Guide to Understanding Your Symptoms and Reclaiming Your Life*

"Sue Wang has given us a vital memoir of heartbreaking emotional intensity and profound psychological insight. Complex family history, the death of a newborn, illness and healing are stunningly interwoven in *MESSAGES from the Black Recliner*, with universal applications for anyone who wants to grow and deepen."
—Gail D. Storey, author of *I Promise Not to Suffer: A Fool for Love Hikes the Pacific Crest Trail*

"Sue's memoir breaks the stigma of mental health in Asian and Asian American communities. She courageously documents her struggle and recovery from her childhood trauma and the loss of a child. For many women of Asian descent, self-care is a foreign concept. I hope Sue's story will inspire them to take steps to ensure their emotional and physical well-being."

—Karen Shih, PhD, Advisor to Students of Asian Descent and Assistant Dean of Intercultural Education, Wellesley College

"MESSAGES from the Black Recliner is an enlightening stroll through the struggles of chemical sensitivity. This book delves into the body, mind, heart, and soul of painful life experiences and healing from them. Having struggled with chemical sensitivity myself, Sue's words offer hope and encouragement. If you walk with Sue on this journey you'll discover broken pieces of yourself, pieces wanting to be reunited with the whole ... You!"

—Paula Youmell, RN, Wise Woman Nurse & Author

"MESSAGES from The Black Recliner is Sue Wang's gripping memoir that chronicles her journey of nursing her body to health from debilitating chemical sensitivity after discovering that years of unaddressed emotional scars culminated into physical illnesses. The book highlighted how the power of mind-body connection affected many facets of our lives."

—Amy Law, MD, Hematology-Oncology

"This compelling and readable cross-cultural memoir articulates the unconscious impact that childhood trauma can have upon our psycho-spiritual and physical lives as adults, and the way broken-heartedness can translate into devastating physical symptoms. The writing illuminates how the stress of chronic illness can take a toll upon our intimate relationships. May this narrative of Sue Wang's journey to wholeness of body, mind, heart, and spirit be a blessing and inspiration to the many who suffer from inexplicable debilitating illnesses."

—Judy Tsafrir, MD, Holistic Adult & Child Psychiatrist and Psychoanalyst, Harvard Medical School

MESSAGES from the Black Recliner

A MEMOIR OF HEALING BODY AND SPIRIT

Sue Y. Wang

Royal Arch Press
Niwot, Colorado

The names and identifying details of some characters in this book have been changed.

© 2015 Sue Y. Wang
All rights reserved. No part of this book may be used or reproduced in any means without written permission of the author and publisher.

Editor: Jody Berman
Cover Design: Sue Y. Wang. Technical assistance: Noah Glovsky
Interior Design: BookDesignTemplates.com
Author Photo: Stacy Moore

First Edition, 2015
Royal Arch Press, Niwot, CO 80544

ISBN 978-0-9967630-1-1 Paperback
ISBN 978-0-9967630-0-4 eBook

To every light seeker who was once a child.

If you don't accept your body and mind, you can't be home with yourself.

—Thich Nhat Hanh, *How to Love*

PROLOGUE

My son was scheduled to die today. December 20, 1996. The nurse sectioned off a corner of the Neonatal Intensive Care Unit with black drapes. "This way you'll have privacy," Kim said, gazing at us through her deep brown eyes. Her round face and full lips exuded warmth. She gently lifted the tubes and checked the dials around our four-day-old.

"You can take some time with him," she said. "I'll do paperwork next door and will be back."

Teary and freshly scrubbed, Roger and I inched toward Jonah's acrylic crib like we were approaching a sacrificial alter. We had surrendered to our firstborn's subdural hematoma, a severe injury on the brain, causing increased pressure and bleeding.

"He has fewer wires on him than before," I whimpered, pushing my glasses up the bridge of my nose. At least he was not burdened with more tests. I picked up the baby's tiny hand, swollen and motionless since the first hour of his life. Jonah's long, tapered fingers reminded me of those of an angel in an Italian painting. "I'm glad he's wearing the red sleeper we brought." My mouth contorted to suppress the urge to wail. I had imagined a wiggling baby inside the fleece suit when I bought it. Red, a happy Chinese color. A clown tossing a yellow ball was embroidered on the front.

I'll never like clowns again.

"Fewer wires are better, I guess," Roger said, running one hand through his wavy brown hair. He hovered over the bassinette and scanned the newborn's bloated face. Jonah's closed eyes looked like two slashes on a loaf of rising dough.

The digits on the heart monitor above the baby flashed a red 69. The rhythmic beeps, induced by a puffing ventilator, called out some semblance of life. I traced the blue accordion tube from the machine to the baby's mouth.

On paper, Jonah was a vegetable.

Our immediate family had bid good-bye to him. We took group pictures. While holding Jonah, I wasn't sure about smiling to the camera. It was our first and last times together.

"We should let him go so he doesn't suffer anymore," I mumbled.

"Yeah," Roger said and sighed.

Kim reappeared. "I'm going to disconnect the respirator now." She searched our faces.

We nodded, eyes fixed on the mouthpiece.

I clenched my shirt as Kim twisted off the tube from the mouthpiece. The beeps began to space apart. Each pause between the sounds announced the impending death.

Beep. Beep ... beep ...... beep ....

Please take me instead.

For four days I had pleaded and begged for a miracle. Silence from above and bad news continued to mount. No, his brain lost too much oxygen for too long. Yes, you better go see him at Children's Hospital. No, the hiccups you saw were probably seizures. No, there was nothing we could offer him.

The heart monitor digits dropped as Jonah stopped receiving oxygen. 40, 35, 22 ... Hunching over him, my straight black hair fell over my face. I howled with each beep, "Oh no ... no ... NO!" I couldn't feel my chest and yet it connected my arms that arched over the infant cart. My entire body convulsed with despair.

Roger reached for my clammy hand. "This is too much for you, sweetie. You want to wait in the room next door?"

How about I explode?

I had laid in another hospital with a urine bag and stitches in a medicated blur. I clung to what Roger said to me after Jonah was whisked away: *I don't care what happens, I want you.* Other newborns' birdlike cries seeped under the door like poison gas. Each chirp reminded me my child was taken in the middle of the night to be poked and prodded here. Fresh out of the womb, Jonah was a big, peachy baby among preemies in the NICU. He just could not breathe.

"Sue? Want to go to the other room?" Roger put his arm around my shoulder.

I nodded like a toddler. "But he is dying!" I stared at the immobile body once more and backed away. I could not watch.

Roger led me to a square office next to Jonah's station and sat me in front of an empty table. "I need to go back," he said. "You'll be okay?" His shoes squeaked on the shiny, sterile floor as he moved toward the door. I had never seen him weeping nonstop like today. My heart ached at his pain. I ached for Jonah, and the family that would never be.

I nodded to Roger. A life was passing, whether I was present or not. No choice. No logic. My head quivered as I wept in what felt like an interrogation room. I was being forced-fed my son's death.

Is Jonah's spirit here? Is he rising toward the light?

What lesson was I supposed to learn? I was a good person. I was honest to a fault. I got married, worked, and had a baby. Apparently I failed to birth a child correctly. I was infused with a contraction-inducing drug and a high dose of epidural for pain. When I could not push him out, forceps were used. The obstetrician yanked hard, Roger said.

I thought I could *will* Jonah to survive.

After an eternity, Roger appeared in the doorway. "He is gone."

I stood up and hugged him. Both of us were drenched in tears and sweat.

"I smell Dial." A whiff of the familiar brought me to the present. "Why did you use soap?"

"Kim and I bathed the baby."

"How did he look?" A mental picture of our limp, distended child came to mind. I was grateful that one of his parents stayed sane for his transition. My husband endured and took care of each task as they arose. He had split time between two hospitals until I was discharged.

"He looked peaceful." He wiped his long nose with a sleeve.

"Did you use the bunting we brought? It will be very cold where he is going," I sobbed, "in the ... the ground. It's Christmas time in New England!"

"Yes. I know." Crescent-like bags hung under Roger's reddened brown eyes.

Life had gone from jolly anticipation to shattering madness. Postpartum, my head was a fish bowl teeming with thoughts and non-thoughts. Everything had compressed in time. I carried a baby, gained sixty pounds, then he vanished.

"That's good he is wrapped up. Thank you, Rog."

He embraced me and burrowed his head in the crook of my neck.

As a teenage immigrant from Taiwan who learned English swiftly to attend a top college, I was used to doing the work and reaching the goal. I got jobs I wanted despite youth, inexperience. I expected the right outcome.

Not now. Babies die.

It was night and dawn would come. Family was waiting to grieve and comfort. I broke away from Roger to straighten my top. The reflection of my slouching torso in a window irked me.

Get a grip, Sue. You turn thirty tomorrow.

I had seen cruelty before. I could quash my feelings and put on a facade.

It was time to go to dinner with the relatives.

CHAPTER ONE

I flipped out of bed, landing left foot first. Landing was a good thing. My brain had thought the floor was farther away. I grabbed the edge of the mattress and lifted my chest. The white lampshade and night table spun by me and came around. Once. Twice. Again. I reached for my glasses.

I want to go back to normal life. Routine, no drama, able-bodied.

I needed to get to work. The alarm clock on the table displayed 7:12, eight minutes before the set time. A low hum hissed in my ears. I held my temples and asked for stillness, a reprieve from Sue-floating-in-air, the same sensation during our summer vacation and the week after. It was tempting to take off my specs and roll back into bed to oblivion with my companions, Nausea and Lightheadedness.

A week ago I informed my primary care physician that there was no way I was pregnant. She diagnosed vertigo. Sudafed should take care of it in a week, she said.

It did nothing.

The alarm clock buzzed and crashed against my eardrums, sending dismay all over the room. Minutes passed while I pontificated nothing, my head stuffed with cotton balls.

"No-*ah?*" I called to the savior who joined our family fourteen months after we lost Jonah. "Are you up? Time to get ready for school."

No answer. The four-year-old was probably at the other end of the house, in the TV room clicking away on a hand-me-down laptop, drawing pictures for his "business." I shuffled down the hallway with hands on the wall. "Noah," I called out again. "Mommy isn't feeling well. Be helpful. Get dressed for school."

School was Lexington Playcare Center, a highly touted day care facility in our historic Massachusetts town. I had registered Noah two years before he was eligible. LPC's aides socialized younglings with cute activities and noted their bathroom habits or lack thereof. My son fell in the latter category. He did not seem to be in a hurry to get out of Pull-Ups.

I am in a hurry. I opened my mouth to holler, to let out the unwellness and frustration, but I closed it. After losing Jonah, I was more conscious of the privilege of motherhood. I gave up a management job in career services at a college to stay home with Noah. Now, two years later, I worked as a part-time childcare researcher. I got to commune with adults, earn a salary, and provide health insurance for the family. It was a better balance than my typical all-or-nothing approach to doing things.

I padded barefoot through the kitchen to the TV room. "Here you are. Close the computer. You can come back to it later."

"Few more minutes," cherub-cheeked Noah said.

"Come on." I rested my head on the paneled wall across his table. After counting to ten I took his hand and walked him to his room. He picked out a navy blue T-shirt and shorts, his standard issue.

"Let's see how fast you can go, like a racing car," I smiled. "Come on."

Noah pulled on the shorts. I left to get breakfast and pack his lunch. Outside the kitchen window, the August sun sparkled behind dense foliage in the backyard. The light bounced with a breeze, which was blinding to a vertigo mind. I turned and held on to a shelf as I fished out a box of Cheerios.

"Your food is ready." Like beckoning a pet, I put out milk-soaked cereal in a plastic dish. The mushy consistency was what my geriatric preschooler requested.

Noah climbed onto the chair and picked up the spoon next to the bowl. "Mommy, I want to stay home."

"Sorry, buddy. It's a school day and I haven't been at work for two weeks."

Noah attended school three full days a week. Nine hours was a long day for a little one, but I wanted to minimize the one-hour roundtrip to Wellesley by working fewer days. I petted his feathery brown hair. "You are going to visit the fire station, remember?"

My son gazed at his dish.

"We're going to be late." *Let's go, kid,* I frowned. I sat next to him and propped my head with one palm. We had covered the hardwood dining table with a new vinyl tablecloth. Bright lemons, dark red apples, and blueberries were imprinted on its matte surface. Its odor gave my mouth a sweet tang. I put my head on it and closed my eyes. *Maybe I should call in sick again.*

No. I was a professional.

"Can you make it easier for Mommy, please? Eat," I mumbled to the tablecloth.

"Mommy, do I have to go to LPC? I want to stay home." He leaned over the bowl and took one spoonful.

"I need to go to work. Your teachers and friends are waiting to play with you." A tinge of shame from standing at the back of my first-grade classroom invaded my fuzzy mind. I was only two minutes late. No way would I let that happen to Noah or me. I sat up. "Move it, buddy." I squeezed out a grin-grimace.

Noah smoothed over his teeth with his tongue. Before. Each. Bite.

He needed his food, I told myself.

When his bowl was empty, my queasiness was everywhere. In the head, chest, and stomach. I drew a deep breath. Breakfast was not happening for me. Better to keep moving. I pushed myself up from the table.

We descended the wide staircase to the front door. The wrought iron handrail's cool sturdiness felt safe under my hand. It was a contrast to the heavy, shapeless air outside. There was no place to hide from the Boston summer. It owned us. I buckled Noah into the backseat of the station wagon and slid in the front. Humidity surrounded my head and I squeezed my eyes shut. The voice of one of my bosses, Wendy, rang in my ear: "Sue! I don't want you to drive when you are dizzy and crash on Route 128."

Oddly, my head was not spinning now, just foggy. Good enough, I reasoned. I did okay getting home from the grocery store yesterday.

I fired up the ignition.

~

"Mom-my, the speed limit says thirty-five and you are going forty," my early reader declared behind me. His specialty was numbers, speedometers, clocks, and anything that spun. Ceiling fans and wheels.

"You are right. Mommy is going fast. It's not good." I glanced at the rearview mirror to meet his big, earnest brown eyes. "When you are thirty-six and a father, you can decide whether to go over the limit once in a while." It was one way to rationalize adult transgressions.

After Noah signed in at LPC, I had twenty minutes to make the thirty-minute drive to work. I buzzed down the windows and steered toward the highway. Cars merged and flew by like Olympic speed skaters as I vied for a space in the traffic. Good, I remembered how to do this. I savored the wind flapping on my face and hair until a gawker-blocker, an accident on the opposite side, halted the flow. As I inched along in rush hour, my grip on the steering wheel hardened. I worked with moms who understood the impact of children on timeliness. Still, I needed to do better.

I arrived at Cheever House, a dignified mansion enclosed by rhododendrons and azalea bushes. A mile away from the Wellesley College campus, where my old job was, the converted estate accommodated researchers on women's issues. The building appeared the same as I had left it. Somehow that was a surprise. I got out of the car and yanked my black ankle-length dress off the seat. It hung loose on my five-foot-six body.

I run-walked to the entrance. Hints of hot asphalt greeted my nose.

"Hi, Jane." I blew by the receptionist and headed toward the third floor, two steps at a time. The air got hotter and thicker as I ascended. Cheever had no cooling system. A few weeks ago we were sent home early because of the poor air quality during a heat wave.

Reaching the door of my shared, cavernous office, I panted and steadied my head. Inside, my colleagues surrounded a folding conference table discussing data consistency.

"Welcome back." Wendy, a research scientist, nodded when she spoke. Her auburn hair complimented her fair complexion.

I entered to address four pairs of eyes. "Sorry I missed the start of the meeting. I couldn't get out of the house this morning."

"How's the vertigo?" Wendy asked and shuffled a stack of surveys in her hands. "You drove yourself?" She was the resident mother of the office.

"I'm a little hazy, but I managed," I replied. "The Sudafed isn't helping, though." I wasn't going to say that I drove Noah. "Sorry I was late."

"It's okay. We're glad you are here. Let's continue the meeting," Wendy said.

I sat down with a pen and a pad. Wendy's voice, like the chimes from the grandfather clock downstairs, began to dissipate into space. I looked at each face in the group—mellow, pleasant. Like the lush pasture outside our wall-size windows. Warm, heavy air surrounded me like bubble wrap, separating me from the others. I heard things like *data cleaning, analysis,* and *regression.* Eventually people got up.

"Sue?" Wendy tapped my arm. "You should go home. You are frowning and you look green."

CHAPTER TWO

"Zoo ... yoyo ... xylophone, ..." I called out from the round black tent. I was told to focus on a red dot projected in front of me and think of words in reverse alphabetical order. The chair to which I was strapped began to spin, and I floated in blackness. My pulse raced against the wristbands that secured me to the seat. I was at the Jenks Vestibular Laboratory of Massachusetts Eye and Ear Infirmary, getting tested for ear and balance diseases. A month of nausea and vertigo landed me in this apparatus.

"Wind ... van ..."

"I'm turning off the red dot," Donna, the technician, announced through a speaker.

Prone to motion sickness as a child, I used to throw up on airplanes. The dot gave some context of my physical existence. After it disappeared, I felt blind. The disorientation sent me dry heaving as the chair rotated faster.

Panic filled my chest, and icy pricks sprang up all over my arms.

I don't know where my body is. It's too closed in here.

"Unicorn ... tape ..."

Spin the patient with the balance problems. It was like giving someone poison to see if she would die. I needed to withstand this so the doctor could figure out what was wrong.

"Stone ..."

Panting became short of breath. I had nightmares about being trapped in falling planes. My dank fists clenched. The darkness around me was choking.

"Road ..."

Vomit threatened to spill out of my throat.

"Q-Q-Queen. Stop—please stop!"

The chair slowed to a halt. Donna turned on the light and slid open the fabric around my chair.

I gasped. "I didn't know I'd hyperventilate ... I've gotten sick but not this," I told her. "Sorry."

Dressed in a white lab coat, Donna undid the straps on my ankles and arms. They were to prevent me from falling out of the chair. My mother used to tie me to a bamboo chair when I was a toddler. She did not want me to fall out either.

Donna handed me a paper bag. "Breathe into this." She stared at my face to make sure I was okay.

Paper bag over my nose and mouth, I tried to rein in my runaway pulse. *What an idiot.* I flunked the spinning chair test. Some people, like Roger, would have loved it like an amusement park ride. I thought these ear tests would be easy. The one before this involved my standing with a parachute-like pack on my back. I shifted my weight according to various stimuli. That was no problem.

"I'm sorry to stop the test," I gulped for air and hoped for sympathy.

"We had patients who couldn't finish. You do what you can," Donna replied with a flat voice. Her piercing eyes shone through horn-rimmed glasses.

"Does this mean that I won't find out what's causing the vertigo?"

"Dr. Jyung will review and discuss the results with you."

Even though my mother had instilled in me to follow doctors' orders, the idea of more waiting bugged me. I had been in the unknown for weeks, and anxiety was mounting like a buzzing ant hill. The only time I felt somewhat okay was being outside. That allowed me to drive to work and shuttle Noah to and from day care.

My breathing calmed, and I informed Donna I was ready. She returned my glasses so I could walk to the exam table for the next procedure. I lay down while she gathered items on a tray from a nearby counter.

It was comforting to be connected to a solid base, grounded to the floor.

"Do you still need these electrodes?" I asked, pointing to the wires attached to my eyelids.

"We use them to track eye movements and the brain's response to the stimulus," Donna explained. She brought the tray near my head. "I am going to put a tiny balloon with cold water in your inner ear, and then a warm one in the other."

I had read about the tests. This one would be a breeze compared to spinning in the dark. Donna's blue-gloved hand came toward my right ear. Then a scratchy sound.

"Oh my!" My innards whirled. I writhed on the table like a severed worm. With the spinning chair test, I could stop the test. Now the source of motion was in *my head*. Eyeballs leaping under their lids, I yelled, "What is happening?"

"The cold temperature in your ear is giving the sensation of spinning in one direction. The warm one should give the feeling of spinning the other way." She waited for me to stop hyperventilating. Having aborted the other test, I was determined to finish this one. I gave the go-ahead for the left ear.

"Ack!" My toes curled. This was the MAX SPIN cycle. Nausea filled my chest and belly. The second time was not any more tolerable. "This is a great way to torture war criminals." I sprawled on the table like a wet noodle, exhausted but glad that the testing was over.

Letting out a faint smile, Donna helped me sit up. "Rest today. We did a lot to your vestibular system."

I couldn't wait to pop some Ativan prescribed by Dr. Jyung, the ear, nose, and throat doctor, and sleep off the adventure in high-tech diagnostics. The drug would put me in a daze, and I would not be dizzy *or* alert. It would be a temporary fix before lightheadedness resumed. I knew because I had used it after work and on weekends. Dr. Jyung had prescribed the drug two weeks earlier after a failed attempt to reposition my ears to correct the vertigo.

I grabbed my bag on the chair across the exam table. Above the chair was a large, detailed drawing of the inner ear. I had studied the illustration online for days, trying to understand conditions of the ear and cranial diseases. I cringed when I read how an acoustic neuroma, a tumor on the ear nerve, is removed. Through the nose.

I had a child. I could not be punctured in the head or taken apart.

I held on to the wall and opened the door to the waiting area.

"How was it?" Roger stood up from his laptop and piles of paper. His striped shirt and khakis creased from sitting the whole morning.

"Terrible." I fell into his arms. "I couldn't finish one test. I hope the doctor can still figure out what's wrong."

He put a warm hand on my shoulder. "Glad it's over," he said.

After he collected his things, I followed him across the office, zigzagging in my tracks.

~

I spent next week recovering from the vestibular tests, and got back to my "old" level of lightheadedness. We drove to Dr. Jyung's office on a sunny day. Through the passenger window I admired people along the Charles River enjoying a nice September afternoon. They seemed so free and I wished I was one of them.

"It's good that my colleague connected me to her fiancé who's an ENT—good to know him personally," I said, still gazing out the window. My mother revered doctors and often took me, my younger sister and brother to an internist. My medical file at that office was an-inch thick by the time I was seven. "Finally we'll get some answers now. This guy should be able to help me." I folded my hands on my lap and glanced at Roger.

"This is a world-renown hospital, Sue. We are lucky to have access to it." Roger turned to me. "It's been over a month that you are not functioning," he said.

"I know."

"You've been unhappy—"

I wished he would keep his eyes on the road. "If you woke up every morning exhausted, off-balance, and sick, you would be too." I squeezed one hand with the other.

"You yell at Noah a lot." Roger's ringing voice pierced the air between us.

"I get irritated!" The flame in my chest ignited. "He's got allergies. He's a picky eater. He doesn't eat grape skin. His foods can't touch each other. It creates a lot of extra work, you know?" How I resented the innocent soul who came to be with us after our shattering loss. Feeling ill was bringing out the worst in me. I dug my nails into my palms. "Loud kids scare him, and—"

"I got it, Sue." Roger waved his hand. "It's hard to be sick but you shouldn't take it out on him."

"True. But it's not like you are doing much with Noah or household chores." I felt my hip bones protruding under my pants. "I haven't been able to eat. I've lost fifteen pounds. I'm doing the minimum at work."

"This isn't just about you and feeling sorry for yourself. We have a huge mortgage. We switched Noah to a costly private school." Roger's voice grew louder. "I lost my job in January and have to build a law practice from scratch, Sue." He lowered his tone when he said my name, the same inflection he used to train a cat when we dated. "We need to pay bills."

I knew our predicament. Fretting about money was in my genes. I was simply overwhelmed, not looking for pity. Illness was front and center, first and everything, every day. "Turn here," I urged, pointing to the black-and-white parking gates of the Mass Eye and Ear.

We got off the parkway. Roger wedged the car into a space in the crowded lot. We moved in silence on cracked concrete sidewalks, and I welcomed the break from our exchange. Orange signs and plastic nettings directed pedestrians through an obstacle course to the entrance. Inside the hospital, we passed by patients with bandages over their eyes, nose, or ears, some in wheelchairs. I hoped not to end up looking like one of them.

"I'm getting lightheaded," I steadied myself against a wall. My body could not feel gravity. I was spacewalking.

We entered the elevator to get to Dr. Jyung's office. When we exited, I scanned the gray hallway. Empty, nothing suspicious. Roger put his arm around my waist in case I lost my balance.

"Your MRI looks good." Dr. Jyung leaned back on his black padded chair. I gazed at the radiant face of the young doctor. His glasses gleamed under the fluorescent light. "There is no tumor on your acoustic nerve."

The muscles on my face loosened. The suffering in the closed, banging MRI tunnel for an hour was worth it. I squeezed Roger's thick hands in the seat next to me. He squeezed back.

"What about the vestibular tests? Was it okay that I couldn't finish one test?"

"Yes, that was all right." Dr. Jyung fanned out several pieces of papers on his desk. "From the lab results I can't tell if there is anything wrong with your balancing mechanism. It looks like everything works in a reasonable manner. Your hearing is excellent, even with the humming." He nodded to us.

"What?" I muttered. That should be good news. But then what was wrong with my head? Dread began to fill my veins.

"We call this kind of result 'nonspecific.' At this moment, there's no clear cause to your symptoms." He folded his arms across his chest, and his tone conveyed confidence.

"You don't know what's making me dizzy?" My brows rose above my glasses. I turned to Roger, who pressed his lips together.

"Not at this point. There are more intensive tests we can do if things don't improve in three months. You can take the Ativan I prescribed as needed. Rest and see if you feel better. Sometimes these things resolve over time."

"Ativan can be addictive," I said.

"Yes. You can take Benadryl. It might dry up the fluid in your system. Maybe that would help."

I knew Benadryl did not work for me. I was not big on taking drugs indefinitely based on a doctor's guess anyway. This young, polite ENT, a fellow at the Infirmary, would likely do well in his career. But he could not help me.

"Thank you," I said, and shook Dr. Jyung's hand. We left his office and headed toward to the elevator.

"Rog, what do I do about my dizziness?" I shrilled. "What the hell is 'nonspecific'?"

"Calm down, Sue. We are in a hospital," Roger scanned around us. "Getting mad won't help."

It was the only thing I could do. I jabbed the elevator button with a stiff index finger. I had tried drugs, ear manipulation, had blood tests for all kind of diseases. Being *sick* sounded all encompassing, one-dimensional, like the sky was blue. The reality was, I was sick, with a young child, a husband, a job, a loss, a life history. Everything had to continue with the illness. The frustration in me screamed *When does this end so I can relax?*

I was broken, and I was tired of me.

CHAPTER THREE

The home inspector who met us at our front porch coughed and gagged. "Are you wearing a down jacket?" he asked Roger through his fist.

Roger fished out his keys from a puffy blue jacket. "What? ... Down?"

"Yes," I answered for the inspector, "he said 'down.'" I stepped toward Jeff May. "Are you allergic to it? Should Roger take off his coat?"

"I'm deathly allergic to feathers," he said. The author of *My House is Killing Me,* Jeff gasped as condensation in the cold October air rose around his face. "Please take it off ... *cack-cack* ... Put it away while I'm here."

Roger unlocked the door and stripped off the offender. In the hall closet it went. That stopped the hacking.

"We moved here fifteen months ago," I said. "I was fine until the end of this August." Standing in our slate-lined entryway, I braced for nausea.

Two weeks ago, a week after the nonspecific diagnosis from Dr. Jyung, we packed up to stay at my brother-in-law's home half an hour away—in case our house was the problem. Indoor mold had made the news in the record-setting hot summer of 2002, and people reported ruined properties, respiratory infections, and headaches. This news had me include indoor home pollutants in my research. I had been on the internet learning about balance diseases, and camping out in the health section at Barnes & Noble, where I found Jeff's book.

I rubbed my hands for warmth in our unheated home. A sad longing rose to my throat. We led Jeff to the utility and storage room across from the front door. Roger flipped a red switch on the gray-blue furnace, and it roared to life. A blue flame danced inside the metal box.

"This furnace seems clean and fairly new," Jeff said, leaning toward the labels on the appliance. "How big is your house?"

"A little over twenty-eight hundred square feet," Roger said, walking closer to the boiler.

"This unit is overkill. It can heat four thousand square feet," Jeff explained.

"Is that a bad thing?" I asked. Lightheaded, I rested my head on the rough wood paneling. My temples tightened. Queasiness invaded me like a guerrilla fighter. Stealth and fierce.

"It's not bad, just inefficient. It warms up the whole house quickly, turns off and fires up again when the temperature drops below the setting. It goes on and off instead of staying on, and spits extra gas each time it ignites."

Extra gas.

I pushed my toes into the floor to make sure I was on the ground. "I get whiffs of gas when I come in here. I assumed all furnaces smelled like that." The invisible and combustible entity always unnerved me. I was a sniffer. Once I amazed the gas company by finding a leak before a technician applied bubble-testing solution to the pipes. In childhood, a neighbor tried to kill herself with gas. At the last minute she banged on our door for help, which I opened. The fumes filled the shared stairwell.

"Can gas cause nausea?" I asked.

"Not enough to give you severe symptoms. It dissipates. This is an older house, not so tightly constructed." Jeff walked the perimeter of the room. His dark taupe canvas jacket contrasted his peppered curly hair. "Popcorn ceiling, old linoleum tiles ... what kind of wood is this paneling?" He pointed to the three walls surrounding us.

Roger slipped his hands in his jean pockets. "I don't know, but the previous owner did a lot of work on the house.

"Looks like pressure-treated wood, which is preserved with arsenic to prevent rot. It's meant for outdoor use.

You might want to ask the people who sold you the house to confirm."

I jumped away from the wall.

It made sense that a professor of economics, a thrifty New Englander, would use indestructible material for this room. I stared at the green-tinged wood. Arsenic. Thanks, Yankee value-consciousness. After losing Jonah, I would not take any chances with Noah. "We have to get rid of this. It's poisonous—bad for a child, if not for all of us," I implored.

"I'll check on that," Roger said.

Sickness flooded me. "I need air. Be back." I ran toward the front door. Once outside, I panted with slumped shoulders. Across the street, white smoke floated out of the chimney of a brown split-level. A couple had raised three children there. Their grandchildren played in the manicured yard and rode bikes in the cul-de-sac. I had hoped we could settle here like them.

I turned to our steel-blue raised ranch. Its backside sat against a knoll, which was solid feng shui, a Chinese system of balancing energies to support the wellbeing of dwellers. As someone who was hopelessly nearsighted, I was struck by the light that poured through the wall-to-wall glass when we first saw the house. There was wood under old brown carpets, which we could refurbish, and baseboard heating. No air ducts—perfect for Noah's dust mite allergies. The house had the potential of clean and bright, a relaxed joy. On a half-acre lot, it offered solace, unlike our oppressive, low-ceilinged first house. I had lost Jonah there, and our yard had become overrun by neighbors' unleashed dogs.

To pool funds for a larger property, I had quit going to therapy after a year and gave up applying to a doctoral program in education. We bought this place at near asking price despite needed updates and repairs. We took on over half a million dollars of debt, sanded the floors, cut down trees. We invested time and energy. Despite such efforts, the house did not seem to belong to us. We moved out after I got sick. It felt like sustaining a pregnancy but unable to keep the baby.

I shook my head to rid its wooziness. The more I thrashed, the dizzier I got.

The house, with its two wings and a pitched roof in the middle, looked like an airplane taking off. A nice omen for a new beginning. I loved its open floor plan, gleaming floor, and a yard where I cared enough to plant blue pansies for Noah. For someone who grew up in crowded cities in Taiwan, this place was luxury. I had a study of my own, which I filled with shelves of books and my collection of thumb toys.

As a child, I yearned for a stable, permanent nest amid many moves and parental arguments. My skittish heart had shunned committing to a place called home until now. Maybe a part of me still felt undeserving. Our widowed seller thought so. She reportedly threw her keys on the table at the closing because she did not get her asking price. She, an established author, left in the living room a huge poster of herself when she vacated the house.

Had we made a mistake buying this place? We were stuck with it now. When Roger inquired with a broker about selling it, she asked if something was wrong with it since we hadn't lived there for long. He replied that I didn't feel well and we didn't know if it was the house. The call ended with the realization that we had to take care of whatever issue hidden in the home, since we wouldn't sell it with undisclosed problems.

After staying away for a week, I felt a little better. My head was not floating in air all the time, and the nausea relented. Could the problem be our house, my head, or both? I was afraid to learn the answer even though I needed one.

I surveyed the sky. The treetops had turned amber and gold, and began to bare themselves. A few dried leaves crunched under my boots and fell to pieces.

If you are here, Jonah, please send me a sign. I'm losing my mind.

I believed in spirits. I grew up worshipping the dead. Maybe my son was watching over me.

Nothing from Jonah. And I thought I was special. I thought I was anointed with immunity from hardships after surviving his loss. I had attempted to replace one child with another. I hoped for another boy so I could do everything right the second time. My wish was granted. What else did I want?

Sighing, I went back inside to hear Roger and Jeff upstairs in the living room. The inspector's voice boomed under the cathedral ceiling. "Oh no. These chairs are stuffed with down. E-h-h ... ahh-*choo!*"

I ran up the stairs. Jeff put a hand over his mouth and gestured at a pair of stained, gold upholstered wing chairs and a striped Queen Anne couch, courtesy of Nana, Roger's deceased grandmother.

"I'm sorry, Jeff. Do you need to leave the room?" I worried he would vomit or pull a hernia. How could someone so allergic investigate the perils in houses? Jeff was the canary in the mine.

He shook his head, still pointing to the chairs, "I'm okay."

"You sure?" I asked. "Is the furniture that bad? Should we throw them out? How come I don't have reactions to it?"

"Different people have different allergies. Dust mites live in feathers. Their feces become toxic with mold. Over time pillows or cushions become heavy with waste, heavier than the down itself." Jeff rubbed his nose.

"I remember the pictures from your book." Black drop-shaped bugs with spiky legs. We owned down comforters and pillows. I got zippered fabric covers to keep the beddings encased.

"Do you think the down is contributing to my nausea?"

"Not necessarily. Usually we see respiratory symptoms like bronchitis or sinus infections."

"Sounds *nonspecific* to me." My voice registered an octave higher.

"Sue." Roger stared at me, trying to prevent me from saying something flip.

A few days earlier Jeff's associate had found a patch of mold in our downstairs closet, which he deemed not enough to cause illness. We paid more for Jeff to do a thorough assessment. It was starting to look like a witch hunt.

We shuffled to the bedroom wing and filed into a hallway. Jeff shut the doors to the living room and three other rooms. "This is my favorite part of the house," he said. "See, there is nothing suspicious here. No air ducts, intakes, carpeting. Feels clean."

I should sleep here.

Jeff scanned for mold after we proceeded to the master bathroom. He did not find rotting or soft areas under the tiles. I asked him if there were too many chemicals in my collection of shampoo, gel, and hair spray. The night before I first woke up sick, I had primped and processed myself for a family wedding.

He bent over the products and inhaled. "I smell some fragrance. Doesn't seem bad. I'm pretty sensitive to chemicals."

One thing off the list of possible culprits from my research.

Roger and Jeff went out to scrutinize the exterior of the house. I overheard Jeff saying critters probably lived under our previous owner's do-it-yourself addition, now Roger's home office. The bottom of it was covered with insulation, but was not sealed off from the elements and provided a home to rodents. The office was next to the master bedroom, and animals could traverse the entire house from there. Accumulated waste in floors and walls would collect mold and toxins. With the hot, steamy summer, bacteria could rise to our bedroom.

After Jeff collected indoor air samples to test for toxic mold, we bid him good-bye.

Sitting at the lower part of the stairs, I looked up at Roger. "No smoking gun so far," I said, sulking. "You think chipmunk poop can make me dizzy and brain fogged?"

"It's hard to believe. Even if there're some, it would be contained in the walls and floors. Let's see if Jeff finds something in the air samples." He sat next to me. "I'll just have to replace the insulation and seal the bottom of the office."

To do that Roger would have to bend low in a crawl space for hours. We did not have the funds to hire helpers.

"I know you are working a lot. Thank you. These are tough jobs." I rubbed my aching head. "I hope Jeff doesn't find toxic mold. But I kind of hope he does." A known foe was better than a concealed one.

CHAPTER FOUR

My temples tightened as the sirloin got tossed over the flames. Thin, marinated meat crackled on the hot black grill. It oozed a sweet garlic aroma after a loud *zzzz*.

Patrons in the Korean BBQ restaurant crowded around built-in grill tables, their heads bowed over spicy ribs, stir-fried vermicelli, and hot soup.

"Thanks, Howard and Esther, for letting us stay with you." I smiled at the couple who sat across from Roger, Noah, and me.

What I wanted to add was, *Would you please vacuum your house?*

Roger glanced up from adjusting the beef on the iron grate. "We appreciate your generosity. It's been crazy. I ripped out paneling and a wall to get rid of pressure-treated wood. Now I'm breaking the ceilings looking for animal wastes."

"Roger, you are my brother. Of course we'd help." Howard's red-brown mustache hid his teeth as he spoke. Beads of sweat shined on his forehead.

Esther had introduced us to the restaurant and it had become a favorite. The scent of roasted sesame oil with pickled bean sprouts evoked a delight from childhood. On occasions I brought my mother, siblings, and friends. Most enjoyed it, except my vegan brother, who called it Mad Cow Country.

Mad in the head. I echoed that. It was a godsend that after one phone call we could evacuate to Howard's home right away. But when I put down our two bags at the refuge and surveyed it, the afternoon light revealed dust balls in corners and under the furniture. According to our home inspector, Jeff May, dust was bad news.

On day one I looked to vacuum. From the hall closet I pulled out a machine and tubes of brilliant chrome. I put it together while Howard worked on a roof deck. I called to him that I would vacuum, and he yelled down that the appliance cost over a thousand dollars and not to touch it. He would do the cleaning. With a racing heart, I disassembled the apparatus and put the pieces away, leaving no trace of disobeying him. The vacuuming did not take place. I never reminded my brother-in-law of it.

"I hope we are not burdening you too much." Roger said, clamping a lump of browned meat and placing it on Howard's plate, then on his wife's.

"It's okay," Esther said. "It's been over a week. I hope you find out what's wrong with Sue." She picked up a leaf of red-laced kimchee with chopsticks. "Do you have any ideas?" she asked me.

What's wrong with Sue. I sounded damaged. I had only suspicions but no answers. I gazed at the blue-orange flame burning under the grill and the flesh above it. My skull felt like it was anchored in a harbor. Something inside was swaying. I closed my eyes.

"Sue?" Esther's voice called in the distance. Her brown hair-framed face came to view.

It must be nice to be clearheaded like her, I thought. She lived in a house where dust bunnies roamed and a thin layer of gray covered dressers. Why wasn't she sick?

"Our inspector is growing mold in his lab to see if we have any lethal varieties. The allergist I saw last week offered me anti-anxiety meds since my blood work looked fine. He said that mold might be the problem." I rolled the BBQ meat into a Romaine lettuce leaf and took a nibble. It did not taste good with nausea.

"Do you feel better in our house than yours?" Esther asked.

"Yes. I'm not as lightheaded as I was at home." *Please vacuum your house.*

I had hoped Roger would raise the issue for me. We had discussed it for a good hour earlier. Seeing his straight back and constant food service to his brother and sister-in-law, I knew it was not going to happen.

~

Back at Howard's, I headed for a shower in the peach-tan family bathroom. The low brown toilet and O-shaped faucets conveyed a modern sophistication in the windowless room. It was a departure from our avocado green master bath that had a view of trees and groundcovers.

The hot water sprayed with gusto. Soon the room was engulfed in white steam. I stepped into the stall and pulled close the curtain. The smell of Korean BBQ rose from my hair. I lathered and squeezed my scalp with my fingertips, wanting to expel my frustration for not speaking up at dinner. I knew that asking for anything was pushing it. Howard, who played the domestic role in his family, had stretched to accommodate us. The overstuffed fridge barely had room for a carton of juice we brought, and the fort-like house remained unlit when Noah and I arrived each night after eating out.

It was enough we had a place to stay.

The water ran off my face. My head went extra light and hazy. I held on to the tiled wall for stability. My breaths quickened. *I gotta get out of here.* I turned off the shower. The ceiling fan hummed but it did not suck out much. One hand on the wall, I swung a leg over the tub and lowered my foot onto the shower mat. The other leg came over as I continued leaning on my hand. After a quick pat with a towel, I threw on my pajamas and opened the door.

"Hey, Howard? There is mold in your bathroom," I called from the doorway.

My brother-in-law stomped down the hall. "I don't think so. I cleaned it before you came."

"There *is* mold. I got really dizzy in the shower. The allergist said mold probably caused the lightheadedness."

Howard stepped into the bathroom and slammed the door.

Head spinning, I sat with cold, wet hair in a chair nearby. The shower roared at a high pitch and water splashed on the walls. I wrapped my arms around my stomach. It was a good thing no one was around. Roger had gone back to clean our house and Noah was downstairs with his cousin and Esther.

The bathroom door flew open. Its overhead light shone over Howard's tall, round frame.

"There is no mold." His bulging eyes radiated behind water-spotted glasses.

"Thanks for checking."

He stormed away.

Do I believe Howard? The inspectors? The doctors? Myself?

I peered into the bathroom. The tiles in the shower sparkled. Each square and its surrounding white grout gleamed with pearls of water. Howard washed everything even though he did not find mold. I had offended him. I should fit into my host's life, not the other way around. According to my mother's voice in my head, needing more from those who already assisted was too much. When I was young we had lived with relatives. Ma implored us to quietly disappear.

As far as I could tell, the difference between my brother-in-law's house and ours was that he had an electric stove instead of a gas one, and his furnace was in the cellar, away from the living areas. Otherwise, I walked under tiny trails of mold on their basement ceiling every day and did not get dizzy.

Maybe mold was not the problem. The allergist said it could be. My eyes welled up. I was a burden to Roger and had just pissed off his brother. How I hated my inability to take care of myself.

I retreated to the guestroom to read my inch-thick *Allergy Relief and Prevention*. Running my fingertip to a bookmark, I opened it. I had read chapters on food and seasonal allergies. None of them said allergies caused nausea. The next section was "What Is Chemical Sensitivity?"

I would skip it. Jeff May spoke with confidence that chemicals were not a problem in my home.

Nah. I should read it.

CHAPTER FIVE

"We need to make changes to our house *now*," I implored from the bed, facing my husband who was sitting on the floor. He had come back to Howard's after working on our home.

"What did you say you have?" Roger asked, rubbing his forehead with his hand.

"Chemical sensitivity. Multiple chemical sensitivity. MCS for short." Tears welled in my eyes. Finally I had information about my condition.

"What makes you think you have this?"

"It's in here." I tapped at the open book on my lap. "I also researched it online. It describes what I feel."

"I've never heard of chemical sensitivity." His weary brown eyes focused on me.

"Me either. I cried when I read it. This is written by an MD. Someone knows about it. I am not insane after all." My heart pounded against my chest. I had to prove something.

"We can't keep spending money on any idea you get. We hired Jeff May, tested for toxic molds, which he didn't find. We just bought a thousand-dollar vacuum to clean the house."

"But it all makes sense—how I had nausea over the new vinyl tablecloth, a stuffed head in Noah's classroom when the teachers were celebrating new carpeting. The snafu with Howard about the shower? The book says it's the chlorine in the water!" My voice shook.

Roger cracked his large knuckles.

I spoke with steady eyes. "We need to get rid of our gas stove and that gas-spewing furnace. Howard's stove is electric and his furnace is sealed away. That's why I don't feel sick here." I pointed to a page in my book. "Look at this."

Roger came next to me and read out loud: "Indoor chemical contaminants: natural gas, vinyl shower curtains, cleaning supplies, particle board furniture, newsprint, chlorine in tap water, printer inks ... Hmm."

The book explained that the brain is the target organ in chemical reactions because it contains a high concentration of fat cells. MCS symptoms include confusion, anger, an inability to concentrate, lightheadedness, emotional instability, headache, fatigue, nausea, and lack of coordination.

"Describes me to a T, don't you think?" I asked and studied his profile. I needed him on my side. Growing up knowing I was a burden to my parents, I had learned to suppress voicing my needs. Requesting what I considered a solution to my ailment was hard. I had hoped a reference book would help me build my case.

"You should confirm it with a doctor. We shouldn't randomly decide this is what you have." He got up from the bed.

"This says chemically sensitive people have an acute sense of chemicals and smell compared to those who are not affected. It triggers anxiety." A tear slid off my cheek.

"Just because you are hypersensitive doesn't mean you have it. You always smell stuff and hear noises." He went back to the floor and crossed his legs.

Yes. I was an alert dog, a light sleeper. My sensitivity and unease had mushroomed since the vertigo. Roger's engineer-attorney-MBA training required evidence that I could not produce. I wondered how I could get his support to start remedying our house. "We need to make changes," I mumbled.

"You are talking about spending thousands of dollars to swap out the furnace and stove. We don't have it, Sue!"

"We have savings. At least change the stove," I pleaded. "It's older and its pilot light is on all the time. It explains why I got extra sick in the kitchen." I wiped off more tears with the back of my hand.

"That's our emergency money." He stared.

I straightened my back and crossed my arms. The book slipped off and thumped on the floor. "Finding ways for me to function *is* an emergency," I insisted.

"Everything is. How do you know changing the stove and furnace will help?"

"I'm not minimizing how taxing this has been for you, but the book says to avoid chemicals like gas—"

"You should find a doctor."

"I have been to every specialist my primary care can think of." Fearing the in-laws would hear us, I leaned near Roger. "I want out of feeling constantly under attack ... I'm desperate. When I get home, I'll throw out everything that contains chemicals."

"I've been working all day, all night on the house. I stooped under it for hours pulling out old insulation and animal carcasses. Give me a break!"

"Have one!" I stood and walked toward the door to leave. "I'll research how much it would cost to replace the appliances."

"Sue ..." The dip in Roger's voice lit a fuse in my chest. Like I was a child. "You should verify this chemical stuff with a professional."

I twisted to face Roger. "Sure. Professionals." I snickered. "One gave me sedatives. Another offered anti-anxiety meds." Four physicians, an MRI, ear tests, blood work, and two house inspectors could not figure out the problem. I turned away and opened the door.

"If you walk out of this conversation, it shows what you think of our marriage."

I stared at the man I loved. This was the guy for whom I converted to Judaism. The guy I craved more time with. We had liked each other.

I pulled the door shut behind me. We had no marriage if I was crazed all the time.

In the adjacent den, the chill of the autumn night settled on the dark floor tiles and shadows of houseplants loomed like ghosts. I plopped in a chair and sobbed.

Everything was wrong. Since we camped out here, Esther announced our stay at every family gathering. Everyone thought my brother-in-law and his wife were great for opening their doors. They were. Though I had hoped for some privacy over our plight.

A few days after we got here, Noah had a bloody fall in school. It required a trip to Children's Hospital in Boston, three floors below where our other son died. My fretting, the illness, and our displacement had affected his sense of wellbeing. The surgeon glued gushes on his chin instead of stitching them. That was a relief. I could not bear having a needle piercing my kindergartener's silken face.

Next to me, Howard's betta fish glided in a bottle on an end table. Its orange tail and fins flared and flowed in the petite container. Fish did not talk or demand. They ate, swam, and if living conditions were wrong, they just died. No negotiations. There was something freeing about that. I pictured the fish going belly up and flushed down the toilet. Death was never far from my mind since Jonah's demise. The possibility of dying scared people into change. If I had a well-known disease, it would be a no-brainer to do what was necessary to improve the situation. But for something called multiple chemical sensitivity, it sounded like a rich person's problem. Random, unheard of, and pricey to mitigate.

I was used to internal panicking. It got me clenching the jaw, grinding teeth at night while functioning during the day. I panicked about my parents going from murmuring to shouting after I went to bed. I panicked about being unable to speak English in a new country when three boys on the school bus molested the only other girl. I panicked when there was nothing to do for a brain-dead son. The kind of panic I felt now was different. Doing it all inside myself was not enough.

CHAPTER SIX

The next day I went shopping to replace some personal items. Little things. No more chemicals, I told myself. I hoped to find what I needed at Whole Foods in Bedford, a little farther away than our usual grocery store. I had never shopped there before. Sadly, Jonah's grave was on the way. As I drove by the cemetery, I recalled throwing a shovel full of dirt over his tiny white casket adorned with a wooden Star of David. I swallowed some tears. This MCS was pushing me to do new things, like toughening my psyche by passing Jonah's place en route to somewhere else instead of making it a destination and bawling there.

The energy of Whole Foods was cheerful. Bright sunflowers and verdant potted plants welcomed customers near its entrance. My mood shifted from gloom to curious. On aisles in the Body section, small jars, boxes, and bottles invited attention.

A teenager wearing a green apron with CARMEN on the right corner stepped in front of me. "Can I help you?" No one could so far. I shifted my weight from one hip to another.

"I'm looking for personal care stuff?" Fresh from a stop at my house dumping hair spray, perfumes, still-shrink-wrapped makeup from Clinique, I was giddy in a lightheaded way. "I just turned chemically sensitive." It was the first time I owned the label to a stranger. Carmen's lucid eyes and rosy cheeks exuded health. I wished I had her glow.

"Chemicals? Which chemicals?" She flipped her brown hair behind her shoulder.

The book I showed Roger had a list of no-no's but I couldn't remember all of them. My neck and armpits burned. "Hmm ... no petroleum-based products?" I felt like a fraud.

"We carry all-natural products. Sometimes people have allergies, so I have to ask." Carmen pointed to a shelf. "Here are face soaps."

I grabbed Alba Vitamin C Facial Cleanser, derived from coconut, orange, and vitamin C, things I recognized. "Looks good. I have been dizzy a lot." I searched on Carmen's face for something. I did not find it. "Do you have lipstick?"

She turned to the next aisle. I followed her to a wood-framed counter with cotton swabs and a ceramic basin that screamed plain and exquisite. She pointed to clear trays of tiny pots and packages. "There are many brands. We have a German line that's really nice."

German probably meant expensive. "I want something simple and not pricey—I've chemical sensitivity and have to replace all my stuff," I said.

She handed me a box of slim golden tubes with pink and burgundy tips. "Burt's Bees is a good brand. Here are samples."

I put the carton on the counter and pulled out a lipstick. "Thanks. I'll be here reading ingredients. You'll see me again, for sure."

She smiled and disappeared.

For some reason I wanted to befriend a store clerk. What was wrong with me? In the gray morning, most people were at work. I stood in the middle of the empty aisle; my head buzzed with the fluorescent lights above. Around me was an endless floor of products under a high ceiling. I was on my own island. Alone.

~

Two nights later, I informed Roger it would cost four hundred dollars to switch our stove from gas to electric. "Could we start with that?" I leaned on the doorway in our temporary bedroom at Howard's. "We've been staying here for almost a month. We should go home."

"We should. Did you get confirmation that changing the stove is what we need to do?" Sitting on the bed, he looked up from his laptop.

"Why is my saying so not enough?" I frowned.

"Because you aren't a doctor. You said your problem was caused by mold before." Roger pulled at his baseball cap.

Déjà vu. Blood pounded at my temples.

"An allergist, a *doctor*, suggested that!" I shouted. I listened to one doctor who was wrong and I was stuck with the mistake.

"We don't have enough information to make a decision," Roger sneered. "Don't use an angry tone at me. I grew up with that."

We all had wounds from childhood. The tone in my voice bothered him, and feeling unheard irritated me. I rolled my eyes, trying to keep it down a notch. "I don't have a doctor for MCS yet. Since I can't fix the chemical sensitivity, I'm going to fix the varicose veins." I pulled up my slacks to reveal clusters of green-blue blood vessels on both legs. "I've been in pain with these for two years. You've seen me having trouble sleeping when they act up." The condition worsened after each pregnancy.

Roger ripped off his cap. "Are you getting even because I'm not agreeing to change the appliances?"

"No!" I dropped the pant legs. "I need to do something to feel better. I saw a surgeon last month. The ultrasound showed the veins have lost elasticity, causing bad circulation." My voice trembled. "He will strip the veins in the right leg first, and the other later. Insurance will cover it."

"This doesn't make sense. You are already sick with something else." Roger shook his head.

"Does to me."

I had found a brochure on chemical sensitivity in a health food store that said the afflicted needed to modify lifestyle to manage the condition, and take care of oneself. Since I couldn't do the former, I was doing the latter.

CHAPTER SEVEN

In the four-by-four changing room at Mount Auburn Hospital in Cambridge, I kneeled.

Dear The One Above, I'm humbled by Jonah's death and health problems. Please help me have a successful vein surgery, go home, and be with my family in peace. Let me turn the corner, get better for good. I am grateful for any assistance.

I stuffed my red sweater, gray sweatpants, underwear, and socks in the clear "patient belongings" bag. My left hand was free of the gold wedding band and ruby diamond engagement ring. Roger called it the princess ring—its red and colorless sparkle symbolized our mixed-race union.

I was a body, unaffiliated to anyone. Fasted, emptied, and raw for anesthesia. I lay under a sheet on the white operating table and a nurse wheeled me into the hallway where Roger and I exchanged a quick peck on the lips. He wished me good luck. "See you in an hour," I waved.

The windowless corridor made it impossible to discern the time or where I was. It was a tunnel to nonexistence. I had signed the hospital papers acknowledging that general anesthesia could result in death. At the pre-op appointment a week before, I mentioned to the medical staff I was sensitive to chemicals but no one showed concern. Dr. Davis, the surgeon, had pushed for the general anesthesia, said he did not want me to "wake up in the middle of the surgery." MCS was new to me and with my doctors-know-all upbringing, I nodded.

"Everything will be fine," he assured me in the Operating Room. "You're going to love the results." Dr. Davis's cheer scared me a little.

Four medical residents crowded at my side. I had agreed to let them observe the vein excavation. A nurse injected into the IV in my wrist.

"Rubber bands snapping ... hear that?" I lifted my head from the table. "Do you hear that?" I repeated.

Four faces looked at me, at each other. They were expressionless.

"No?" I asked. The nurse removed my glasses. I blanked out.

~

"Ohhh ..." I woke up behind a shell-pink curtain. A woman in blue scrubs sat beside the bed.

"How are you?" she asked, leaning over.

"I am nauseated," I moaned.

"We'll give you something for that." She got up from a rolling stool and walked out.

I dozed in a haze and tried to swallow the discomfort. What was that snapping sound I heard before the surgery? And why did I feel so badly? The surgeon didn't say the procedure would have such an effect.

"The surgery went well." Minutes later, Dr. Davis stood over me and smiled. "We removed the clumps near the knee and stripped the large vein from your groin to the ankle." Keep it wrapped and I'll see you in a week." He disappeared from view.

The nurse returned with a syringe. "It's anti-nausea medication. It'll help you feel better," she declared and shot into the IV line.

Coolness spread through my arm as she administered the drug. "I'm chemically sensitive ..." I drawled. I wasn't sure if I was heard.

"I'll check on you soon." She walked away.

Roger's concerned grin appeared. "How are you doing?"

"My leg's okay." I showed him how it was bound in a bandage like a mummy. "But I want to throw up."

"Want me to get the doctor or nurse?"

"Could you ask the doctor what they just gave me? I tried to tell the nurse I'm chemically sensitive. She acted like she didn't hear me."

Roger left. When the nurse came back, I told her I did not feel better. She infused more drugs in me. It took four hours in the Recovery Room instead of the one we expected. I held off the nausea in the car on the way home. We had replaced the kitchen stove and returned from Howard's two weeks ago. I was glad, with apprehension.

~

We slept under the chandelier in the dining room. It was the farthest from the chipmunk-infested home-office floor. Roger had not finished disinfecting it and replacing the insulation. With the kitchen stove switched to electric, I stayed upstairs, away from the overpowering furnace. Lightheadedness aside, I looked forward to having one good leg. But when I hunched over the kitchen sink to wash a cup, I felt woozier than before the surgery. I lowered myself in front of the cabinet, opened its doors, and checked for bleach and chemical cleaners. Only balls of plastic bags sat under the chrome pipes. I pitched forward and inhaled. The rocking sensation in my head intensified. I sniffed again.

Can't have these in here.

"Roger, please throw out all plastic bags in the house!" I shrilled, as if seeing a monster.

"Why?" He emerged at the kitchen doorway.

"Plastic bags are petro products. They're toxic." I pulled myself up by the countertop.

"Don't raise your voice at me. I told you I don't want it in my life." He bent next to me and yanked out tan, white, and black shopping bags.

"I feel more sensitive since the surgery three days ago."
All I felt was panic. My voice, like my body, was out of control.

"You decided to have an operation even though you have other issues. Don't blame me."

"I'm not blaming. I am trying to feel better."

"I hope you do soon." Roger shoved the bags into the largest one in the pile. "First the bleach and the cleaners get moved to the backyard shed. Now the plastic bags."

"When I'm near them I get more lightheaded."

"You're not making sense. At the hospital you were in recovery for a long time. I kept telling the doctor you were chemically sensitive and he didn't respond. He acted like I was crazy." He grabbed the stuffed bag and ran downstairs.

Appearing "crazy" triggered Roger, who was the youngest in his family and the receiver of unwanted projections. I limped after him.

"*Nothing makes sense* is how I've lived for the last three months," I yelled. "You are not the one who feels like shit all the time!"

Roger re-emerged in the stairwell, nostrils flaring. "Oh, poor you. I live with YOUR problems. I clean up the house, put holes in it looking for animal wastes. We bought a new stove. I have to work to pay for things, you know."

I worked too, three days a week.

"We moved out for a month, put our bed in the dining room. What else do you want, Sue?" His face grew whiter.

"I want to ... *fix* me! What if I feel like this for the rest of my life?" I broke out crying.

"You're such a victim. What are you going to do about it?" Roger screamed.

I had just read online that general anesthesia was lethal to MCS sufferers—I didn't know to research it before the procedure and just went with the surgeon's preference. The drug affected brain, neurological functions. It never occurred to me that conventional meds *were* chemicals.

I hobbled upstairs to my study and slammed the door. Bare tree limbs and the November gray sky drew me to the window. I ogled the ground from the second floor.

Jump. End it.

Condensation from my sobs collected on the glass. I knew death. Suicide was not taboo for me. Growing up, my Ma spoke of "go die" like it was an everyday, viable solution. Her father, a man with a reputation for honesty, killed himself because he was unwell and accused of taking bribes at work. He was spent and ashamed. I resonated with that.

Life was fleeting. Jonah only stayed for four days.

I crammed myself in a corner so the walls would hold me. My head fell in trembling hands and jerked with every sniffle. How did all this start? I did not have a toxic exposure like some people. Did illness just happen? Did I do something terrible? Ma lamented that "being human is to serve for crimes." Life was a punishment. I wanted to believe her now. I fought it all my life as the daughter who loved people and dancing.

I despised Roger's cutting words. But he was right. Just now I felt like a victim. I came from the shadows of oppression, of the powerless. I witnessed a father's cruelty to his family, with no consequence except the spread of fear. Boys were preferred in my Taiwanese culture. Many girls in my parents' generation were given away due to poverty or superstition. My father, Ba, lost a bet that his firstborn was a son when I came. His mother warned him not to name the next child, my sister, with a girl name like Sue, *ladylike* in Mandarin, in order to attract a boy. It worked. My relatives deemed my brother the one who saved my parents' marriage. Fortunately, Ba believed in education for all his kids. I had a masters from Harvard University and a career in educational administration. But when called a victim, a demon was roused.

In the dusk, the hum of my new air cleaner nearby told me of my place on earth. It was the only thing I could count on and allow in my "safe room." Wiping tears with wet, spongy sleeves, I loathed myself for having needs. How could I stand up again? Ma always said, rely on yourself. Long ago, she left after a bad argument with Ba, wanting to kill herself. My father slapped her when they fought, when she was pregnant, when she was not. Her family presumed that was the fate of a woman. "But baby Sue-Yi lying on bed," she told me years later. Ma returned and had more children. Her passive resilience reminded me of surviving as a bottom-feeder, a maggot.

I was not that nor living in Taiwan. A hybrid American and a Wellesley alumna, I took pride in my authority and self-determination. Yet when I pleaded for a new stove and demanded that Roger remove the plastic bags from the house, I felt like the white worm inching over human waste, something I saw as a four-year-old stooping in an outhouse. I defaulted to getting my husband's approval. If that failed, I battled with bitterness. When I got what I wanted, it felt like a handout.

Rely on yourself. Where is my self?

With my opportunities and privileges, I continued the self-disconnect. Deep down, I carried beliefs and wounds of my female kin: Disown yourself, defer to others. I had never questioned the anesthesiologists, surgeons, or obstetricians. I trusted them blindly, like a good girl. I let high doses of drugs flood my body when I was in labor with Jonah. It set up conditions that led to his death. When I had Noah I choked on vomit after a spinal anesthesia. Despite giving "informed consent," I never linked being medicated with the awful consequences that could result. I assumed drugs were routine, and doctors would take care of me.

Self-care was a foreign concept, like it applied to fine-boned, lace-wearing ladies. I was a sturdy-framed Asian woman who did not take time off. Ever since Noah's birth, I slept like a flitting moth, anticipating his every need. I had nursed and hauled his ballooning body with devotion, and tore a muscle in my back. The Perfect Mom wore out in two years. I went back to work. Then I fell ill after helping Ma with her divorce.

I drove my body into a wall.

Noah's face floated to mind. I missed his full, tofu-soft cheeks. Since I got sick, I did the minimum as a mother. I brought him to and from school, fed him mac and cheese, and applesauce from plastic containers. They were his favorite. No vegetables. Fruit without skin. Other than school, he was left in the TV room with a computer. That pleased him too. He loved making art and charts with it. At times I cried, rubbed his head, and apologized for screaming at him. I said I was trying to get better.

The more I fixed my body, the more I botched it. I felt increasingly foggy after the vein surgery, and was shocked to find myself sick near the entrances of CVS pharmacy and Sears. That left few places I could go. If any.

My bandaged leg grew sore. I propped it on top of the air cleaner. The night chilled like the dark slumber in the Operating Room. I scanned the naked walls and empty shelves in the study, everything removed to reduce dust buildup. This room had become a prison.

CHAPTER EIGHT

"Your body is under oxidative stress," Dr. LaCava mumbled under his salt-and-pepper mustache. I found him through an environmental medicine website and scheduled an appointment for a week later. I hoped for a diagnosis and a treatment plan. So far he sounded a bit out there.

"Oxidative what?" I said. High school chemistry was long ago.

Roger leaned forward. "What's oxidative stress?"

"Oxidation. Like a nail rusting. Free radicals are damaging your nerve function. You probably have peripheral neuropathy."

Too many syllables for a muddled brain. "What nerves are you referring to?" I asked.

"All the nerves in your body. We can test your fingertips' reaction time to electric pulses. If nerve endings aren't working well, it'll take a longer time to feel their signals." Sitting opposite us, the doctor was warm in a knowledgeable way.

"How does oxidation relate to chemical sensitivity?" I said.

Dr. LaCava grabbed a folder from his wooden desk. "When the body is under a lot of oxidative stress, it gets very sensitive. It needs antioxidants," he explained.

"Like vitamin C?" My face lit up at the recognition.

"Yes," he said, flipping through my chart. I so wished he would find something that others had missed.

"Doctor, does Sue have multiple chemical sensitivity?"

"If she says she has the signs of it, then she has it," he replied, nodding.

How about that.

I turned to Roger with wide eyes. I *could* diagnose myself—this challenged his and my belief in a doctor's absolute authority.

Prior to the visit, I completed twenty pages of questions on health history, diet, and lifestyle, including whether I used glazed dishes, had mercury fillings, or used tampons. I told Dr. LaCava about the vestibular tests and the latest attack from general anesthesia.

He lifted his eyes from my file. "The most important thing is that you reverse the oxidative process in the body. If you don't, you'll end up with fibromyalgia."

A name that sounded yeasty and difficult. I rested my head on the back of my chair.

Dr. LaCava continued. "We should build you up so you can function again. You can't live in a box. You need to start vitamin C IV and glutathione right away."

When I was little, my mother forced me to get daily shots for half a year. She claimed it cured my childhood asthma. It cured me of needles.

"Can I take the C orally? What's that glu– thing?" I asked.

"Glu-ta-thigh-on. It's a compound that aids liver detoxification, which helps with chemical sensitivity." Dr. LaCava adjusted the stethoscope that hung from his neck. "You must flood your body with a high dose of C intravenously. If you take the pills in the same concentration, your body will pass most of it. In holistic medicine we say 'do no harm' to the patient. Everything I suggest is nontoxic and beneficial."

He pulled a yellow sheet from an acrylic holder on the wall and handed it to me. "Read this on the C IV. I need your written permission to administer it."

Roger tugged at his cap, something he did when he got anxious. "How much is this going to cost and how long would she need the IV?" Dr. LaCava did not take insurance.

"Seventy-five dollars per IV, plus the glutathione. One hundred and twenty. I recommend weekly IVs for a month. Then we'll see how she feels."

Each of these words weighed on my chest like a brick. I searched Roger's face under the shadow of his hat. No reaction.

"Could we have a few minutes?" I said to Dr. LaCava.

"This seems ... so unusual."

He closed the door behind him.

"Rog, what do you think? Does he sound bizarre? Vitamin C IV?"

"He says your body's rusting."

"He already prescribed a bunch of supplements." I held up another sheet where the doctor wrote *MSM, fish oil, vitamin C, vitamin E* ... This is expensive." I reached out to Roger's hand. "I'm sorry."

"You've tried all kind of doctors and that didn't help. There's nothing else to try."

"I hate needles. The money is an issue." I squirmed in the chair.

"I love you, Sue. If it's going to help, do it. I want you to get better."

"For that I'll try the IV," I said. My eyes welled up.

~

Two days later, I drove in a snowstorm to Dr. LaCava's office near Worcester. It took two hours instead of the typical one. The worry about arriving safely distracted my needle angst. After parking in the snow-filled lot, I trudged through slush and slid to the doctor's office.

Elaine, the IV nurse, greeted me. Her blue eyes were tranquil like a mountain lake.

"The walk from the parking lot froze my hands," I said as I hung my jacket on a wooden peg nearby.

Elaine gestured to a chair with a narrow platform in front of her. "Have a seat. Please roll up your sleeves." Her tall stature and soft voice calmed my nerves from the commute.

I sat down. Elaine took my left hand and gazed at the back of it, like scrutinizing an apple at the fruit stand. "Hmm." She chewed her lower lip.

"What's wrong?"

"You have small veins." She took my other hand and examined it. Then she pressed her index finger inside each elbow. "Slim pickings."

I wished I had a third arm. My foot tapped under the chair. I couldn't wait for this magical IV to begin.

She swabbed the back of my left hand. "Here's a stick."

A pop in my skin. The needle burned under the skin searching for a vein. I zeroed in on a poster on the wall. An emerald beach with two palm trees.

Elaine pulled out the needle. "I couldn't get it. Next week, drink a liter of water before you get here and keep your hands warm."

I felt dumb. "Would you like me to run hot water on my hands now, and try again?" I said.

"That would be helpful."

I went to the bathroom across the hall and stood with my hands under the running faucet until they turned pink-red.

Elaine pricked three more places. The alcohol swab sent my head spinning. "Could you use hydrogen peroxide instead? I forgot to say I'm chemically sensitive."

"Yes." She reached for a brown bottle and cotton balls from a box.

I was so glad she knew what I meant.

"I'll try one more place." Elaine wiped the skin on the underside of my lower left arm. Hair stood up on my arms. Where did she want to stick me?

"Relax. Your skin feels tight."

All my organs were tight.

Elaine jabbed the needle into my arm. Pain radiated from the spot. *Ssssss*, I sucked in air through clenched teeth.

"Sorry." She twisted her neck to see the needle. "We have it!"

There was finally red in the catheter. The IV was connected to a blood vessel. I exhaled. The pin cushion portion of the event was over. Elaine taped the IV on my arm and thumb-rolled the control on the line to adjust the flow. For the first time, I saw the bright yellow liquid in a clear plastic sack above me.

"What's this weird taste in my mouth?" It was a cross between rotten egg and metal.

"B-12. It helps with circulation and energy level."

I could use that.

Through a glass door, Elaine led me and the IV pole to one of three green loungers. I eased into the seat as the ache in my arm worsened. I stared at the taped IV site. My pulse sped up.

I can't have a needle there.
It's tender.
I can't have it in there.

The chant repeated in my head. I began panting. My head went light and hands turned cold.

"Dr. La-Cava!" Elaine yelled.

The doctor leaped through the doorway. "Get an ice pack!" He pushed my chair back to the full recline position, and put a cold compress on my forehead.

"Feel better?" He sat next to me.

I nodded, soothed by his olive complexion and deep brown eyes. "I guess I hyperventilate when I panic."

In my whole life I had done this twice, within five months of each other.

"Now we know this about you," he said with a smirk.

Dr. LaCava left after a few minutes. I stared at a pile of magazines on the end table near me. The IV site continued to hurt. Elaine slowed the drip. A one-hour infusion became three. She said that my veins could not handle the acidity. And next time, I should bring water because the IV made patients thirsty. She added the glutathione directly to the IV bag without sticking me again.

I closed my eyes and felt each drop landing on my vein. Ouch. Ouch. Ouch.

I leafed through *People* magazines in attempt to ignore the dull ache in my arm. Three issues later, my bladder was full.

What do I do?

I looked up to see the bag only two-thirds empty. Maybe I could wait until it finished. I was good at holding it—in school, in the car, in shopping malls. The aversion to dirty bathrooms trumped my bodily function.

The cleanliness here was not in question. My comfort about moving with an IV was.

Five minutes passed.

"Elaine, I need to go to the bathroom." It was like I was in first grade.

"Take the pole with you. You can move your arms and hands. Just take it slow."

I saved too much pee to take it slow. I started toward the bathroom and carried my arm at a ninety-degree angle, moving like a robot. Elaine saw my tentativeness and came to push the IV pole in front of me. With the line connecting us, I was a dog she was walking, except I could not lift my leg to go on the brown carpet.

"There. You'll be all right," she reassured and shut the bathroom door.

Trembling with urge, I unzipped my black corduroys with one free hand and plopped down without losing it.

When I finally left Dr. LaCava's office, my hands and arm had four bandages covering the needled sites. I did not feel differently. I sat in my car and sighed, wondering if it was worth all the pain and maneuvering.

CHAPTER NINE

I jumped in the car with a stomach full of fluid. Three goldfish could swim in it. After the trouble I had at my first IV session three months ago, I now drank five glasses of water before each appointment, to the point of gagging. This way my veins would be juicy for puncturing.

I steered the station wagon into commuter traffic like a rat darting for an opening in a stream of rodents. Dr. LaCava also saw patients at Marino Center for Integrated Health in Cambridge, which was much closer than Worcester, but it still took time.

Maybe the adrenaline of rushing diverted my dread of the IVs. Racing off Route 2 and through a light, my car approached Marino's angular building with red-trimmed windows. I scored a parking space behind it. It would save me from feeding a meter during the three-hour infusion.

"Hi-I-am-late." I handed the receptionist a credit card for the copay. Marino Center was a bigger organization than Dr. LaCava's office. It billed insurance for a part of the infusions.

"It's okay, hon." The receptionist's baritone voice and thick eyeliner startled me every time. The voice did not match her petite, gold belt-cinched figure.

She slapped a receipt and my card on the counter between us. I ran toward the stairs next to the entrance. The steps were outgassing polyurethane. I held my breath and hauled my water bottle and magazine up three flights.

"There you are." Diana, the nurse, hung a glass bottle of yellow liquid on a metal pole. Her smile revealed straight, white teeth.

"Sorry." I marched over to the throne, a dark green recliner at the far end of the room. It was a glass enclosure that protruded like a sun porch in the sky. Over the last few months, the high dose of vitamin C and prescribed supplements gave me more energy, so I committed to the treatment on my day off from work.

"Let's see what you have." Diana rolled toward me in a stool carrying a plastic caddy. In it were paper tape, antiseptic wipes, IV catheters, tourniquets, and a rubber stress ball.

I extended my arms for inspection. My heart went staccato. After several IVs, I still could not get used to them.

"Which arm did we use last time? We'll use the other today," Diana said.

"Beggars can't be choosers. As long as you get a vein." I forced out a grin.

"Don't worry. We'll get it." Diana's index finger poked the inside of my elbow. "Here's one."

I felt the cool of the swabbing and turned my head away. The needle stung as it broke through.

In walked Carolyn and Mary, the next appointments. They sat in the remaining recliners near me, opposite each other. I greeted them while the needle searched for a vein.

"I thought I had it." Diana withdrew the device. She fanned out my hand to find another candidate. As long as she did not go to the underside of my lower arms, I was good.

"Here we go," she said. A brown ringlet fell across her face.

I winced with the jab in my hand. "How are you guys?" I called to the ladies to distract myself.

"Tired. I cooked for a festival this weekend." Mary picked lint from her dark plum sweater. Dewy makeup, lacquered nails, brilliant auburn hair. One could not tell she had chronic fatigue. Our afflictions were invisible. We looked okay but felt like ghosts.

"I wished I had your energy to cook like that." I was thankful that my Ma moved in with us after selling one of her small houses. She cooked meals and helped with chores. I had nothing left after work and caring for Noah.

"Got it," Diana announced.

I looked down. Blood rose in the IV catheter. Then vanished. "What just happened?" I asked.

"Your vein collapsed." Diana pulled out the IV. "Let me get someone else." She went next door.

"What collapsed?" I said.

"Your VEIN," Carolyn piped up. She had knitting needles in her hand, ready for her infusion.

"I heard what she said, but what does that mean?"

"The walls of the blood vessel caved in and no blood is coming through." Carolyn was a veteran in the IV Room.

"Oh. I need a vampire."

My friends laughed. We were the Knit and Bitch Club. We met every Friday and commiserated. I was the youngest in the group. Perhaps I had a better chance of bouncing back to health, but it concerned me. I was too young to be a regular.

Diana came back with Vivian from allergy testing, who sometimes doubled as an IV nurse. She pushed her glasses on the bridge of her nose and sat next to me.

"I hope I get lucky with you," I said. I began to sweat in places I didn't know could sweat.

Vivian chuckled and went to work. Her soft appearance was comforting. Curvy hips, rounded corners of her eyes, an OM charm on her necklace. She had connected the IV for me before; maybe today was her day.

"I drank a liter of water this morning." I wanted them to know I came prepared.

Vivian patted the back of my hands for a vein. Two sticks later, she pulled her mouth back to a straight line. "Would you rather come back on Monday?"

"No." I flushed. "I work then. I have to get the IV today. I need to feel better." A month following the first IV, Roger remarked that I "looked like a different person" after a session. Bright eyed and almost cheerful. By the end of a week, I was exhausted. "Please try again. I can't get through the weekend without it." My voice trembled.

I was an addict. Addicted to feeling better. "Would you get Marie?" My eyes went from Vivian's face to Diana's, who had returned after hooking up the other two women. Marie was the phlebotomist who drew blood all day. She had gotten my veins for tests.

"We can try that," Diana replied.

"Thank you so much." I stared at the four pink dots on my arms and hands. Tomorrow their surrounding areas would be black and blue.

Marie strolled in like a queen. Her golden-brown skin shimmered under the overhead light. "Having trouble with the IV?" She spoke with a Caribbean accent. After surveying the inside of my elbow, she wiped me down.

My eyes caught sight of a seagull outside the tinted glass wall. It zipped along the width of the room and disappeared. I traced the glass to the ceiling. A reflection of three nurses' dark heads bending over my arm on a white pillow.

I met my sullen gaze. *This is what it looks like to have a chronic illness.*

Despite the kindness of nurses, love of a spouse, dependency of a child, concern of a mother, it was between me and the Universe. Me and my body. Me against my body. Whatever needed has to come from me *I am it.* I wished I was that bird flying away.

A click of the catheter.

"We got it." Diana broke out in a toothy grin.

"Thank you," I said with a sniffle. "Thank you for the tenacity."

Carolyn and Mary's chatter resumed. I realized the room had frozen in silence during Marie's attempt.

"That's my record—five sticks," I declared, like I accomplished some feat.

"That's a lot, Sue. I'm sorry," Mary said.

I sank into the buttery chair and closed my eyes. From the gum-popping receptionist who called me hon to a group of nurses who flexed for me, this was a different world of health care in which I existed. Here I was cared for, responded to. They treated me as a person, not a body part. The Marino Center became my second home. I was lucky to have found it. Very lucky.

CHAPTER TEN

Run, Sue, run! My knees needed to lift higher. Despite having driven twenty minutes to get to the Wellesley College Sports Center, I was still half awake. Rising early was not my thing. I never got over being suctioned out of the womb at dawn.

Sweating out toxins was good for MCS, and I had some energy from the IVs. Twice a week I crammed in jogging, the sauna, and a shower before work. The red digits on the treadmill displayed 3.4 miles per hour, a wimpy pace. I wanted to sync with the pony-tailed college student flying next to me, but getting sucked under the black conveyor belt would be bad. What the heck. I blipped a button and increased my speed to 5 miles per hour. The motor under me whined a higher pitch.

Inside the sports center, the atmosphere was a blend of frigid and rubber. The faster I ran, the hotter my face. Lightheadedness set in. I held on to the metal bars next to my hips and gulped for air. A little longer and I earned the cool down phase.

A familiar male figure with a blond preschooler emerged at the far end of the building: Hank, the husband of an ex-colleague. His tall, imposing Nordic frame was hard to miss. As families, we went on outings with our strollers of babes. It had been over a year since we saw each other.

Do I say hello? How do I catch up? I usually explained to people how I fell ill and discovered it was multiple chemical sensitivity, what it was, and how I had to live a natural, guarded life. They would cock their heads and frown, saying, "That's terrible, Sue," then politely cut off the conversation because they could not relate or had to go.

I had to go. The large clock on the wall said to hurry. I slept until the last possible moment and carried out my routine with military precision. Every minute was planned. I gazed into the expanse behind Hank as he and his daughter walked near me to leave the area. His eyes registered recognition then he looked beyond me. At that instant I knew I had lost a friendship.

I finished the jog and wiped a tear off my cheek. Having been raised in an unhappy household, I treasured friends. They brought cheer and the privilege of company. They supported and understood. Now MCS pushed the limit of this understanding. Recently a fellow mom showed off her renovated kitchen and I told her the new cabinets made me woozy. She stopped calling. I did not notice. I was too busy identifying offending items to avoid, fretting about getting better, or not getting worse.

In the locker room, hollow metal boxes stood cool and silent. I ripped off my sticky, tight jogging bra. What could I have done about Hank? Our lives no longer aligned—I was the outlier with the weird problem. I threw a towel around me, raced to the sauna, and twisted the knob on the wooden structure to set it for ten minutes. The ticking urged me to get in. Within seconds my skin churned out lines of perspiration, and blood pounded in my temples. Alone, naked in the scorching walk-in closet, I willed the body to withstand. *I am a fighter. I roast in an oven. I breathe and blink fire.* I pictured a warrior princess on a horse slaying enemies. The enemies happened to be in me.

Outside, children's voices rang and feet pattered by the door. It was a Wednesday, and kids in town had swimming lessons here. My skin prickled and ears stood alert.

"Mommy, what's this?" The door swung open. A rush of chill hit my face, invading my self-inflicted torture. A woman and a boy's silhouette entered. I pulled up my towel.

"It's a sauna. It warms you up after the pool," the woman replied. "It's cold coming out of there!" They sat across from me.

The child leaned on her. "What's that clicking noise? Why is it so dark in here?"

My nerves wound with his every word. *It's dark so you don't see lady parts.* We were in a women's locker room at a women's college. It took years to be okay with my nudity. For once I was glad to be extremely nearsighted. Without glasses I could not see faces well enough to deliver a scowl, nor did I feel visible. I concentrated on my back, where long trails of sweat trickled down between the terry cloth and my skin.

The pair left. I was a kid who regained her tree house. I lowered my towel and started to see red when I closed my eyes. There was comfort in feeling the heat, that it extracted venom from a sick body. In solitude, memories simmered. As a young child I was fed a water mixture containing a burned paper talisman from a Taoist priest. It was to "purge fright" and restore calm. I wondered if that would help me now.

The timer's buzz woke me from a stewing mind. I stepped into a shower stall nearby and blasted the water. At home I had charcoal filters attached to shower heads to reduce chlorine-induced dizziness. Here I held my breath, lathered, and rinsed with pulsating speed. I wished my hair was shorter. Its shoulder length took longer to wash but I had no choice. I could not go to a hair salon, where chemical fumes and fragrances reigned. Online I found instructions for cutting my own hair. The shoulder length was what I could muster. About every other month, I sat on a stool, tipped my head toward the floor, and trimmed my tresses for over an hour. A sore neck beat a runaway head.

On my way back to the locker, the zinc-colored tiles shone through smudges of water. I leaned on the balls of my feet so I would not slip.

"Hi." I turned to the green-smocked janitor in white sneakers. Her presence told me I had five more minutes before I'd have to get to work.

"Good morning." She looked up from her mop.

Two feet away, bottles of Pepto pink and blue cleaning agents fill the top of a utility cart.

I better finish before she does.

Boom. She pulled out the metal liner under the paper towel dispenser.

I popped a wet head through a turtleneck.

She rattled the liner to empty it.

I threw on black pants and a red sweater.

She slapped the mop around the toilet stalls.

I smoothed aloe vera gel on my face.

She rustled a garbage bag.

Smearing blush on my cheek ...

Ssssssssss ... sssssssssssss ... She released the perfume bomb. April Fresh raided the room. I sucked in a last whiff of unadorned air.

Many consumer products, as well as construction materials and furnishings, such as printer ink or sprays, emit formaldehyde, an irritating, terrible substance for the chemically sensitive. I did not want to experience fake April Fresh. In high school chemistry we made scents and ethers. Why did humans feel the need to infuse the air with lab compounds? I had contacted the building manager about the air freshener, and the reply was, "It gives an extra sense of clean." Right.

Heart thumping, I threw things in my bag and walked through the fragrance cloud to the door. When I reached its handle, I ran out of the pre-scented breath I had taken. I opened my mouth for air. I read that, if needed, breathing through the mouth could work for MCS sufferers. The bad air would bypass the brain and go straight to the lung.

I burst outside the complex. The frigid air burned my face but I welcomed it. April Fresh had attached itself to my hat, jacket, and newly washed hair. A sweet metallic taste settled at the root of my tongue. The ground beneath me moved and sank. My inhale-through-the-mouth trick did not work.

In the car, the dashboard displayed fifteen degrees Fahrenheit as I headed across campus to work. I opened the windows and my wet hair became icicles. The obstacle course of the morning was completed. I pushed the body hard, like revenge hard.

CHAPTER ELEVEN

Below rolled-up T-shirt sleeves, my arms had hand-drawn grids containing needle marks and pink bumps. I expected to get at least sixty shots today. The spring sun warmed me through tinted glass in the IV Room. The area doubled as a waiting room for allergy testing. Dr. LaCava, with whom I had worked for four months, suggested identifying food and environmental offenders when I got stronger so I could lower the "load" on my body.

Having lots of injections was not as bad as getting one IV. The nurse shot just under the skin, no vein needed. In my palm, a small LCD timer counted down from three minutes.

Please let all food allergy tests results be negative.

For all the nausea I suffered, I still loved food. On a table near me, a glossy brochure listed common allergens: wheat, gluten, soy, eggs, dairy, corn, and sugar. Bummer.

One of my favorite dishes, noodles with soy-stewed eggs and minced pork, called for most of these ingredients. Ma added crystallized sugar in the broth for a nice tang.

And, like Ma, I loved corn in all formats. I ate the cob typewriter style to ensure getting every kernel. I crunched corn chips and popcorn and went into a happy trance. Time stood still.

My mother believed eating well was more important than dressing smart. As her daughter I agreed for the most part. A meal was a privilege. A meal cooked by one of my maternal aunts in Taiwan was heaven. This aunt was known for her delicate shrimp rolls. She chopped water chestnuts, scallions, garlic, and shrimp with a mighty cleaver, and her hefty bare hand blended them with ground pork and spices. My mother, who was much younger, chatted on the side and spread dollops of the pink-and-white mixture on paper-thin wonton skins. The sisters then sent the soft, thumb-size wraps to fry in the wok until golden crispy. The luscious aroma signaled us kids to swarm the kitchen and devour what seemed an endless supply of rolls. We dipped them in sesame soy sauce. After a crunch, the semi-firm stuffing dispersed and melted in the mouth, creating a lifetime of yearning. My aunt encouraged us to eat until the plate was empty.

I wished I could eat those rolls now before I discovered what I was allergic to. The last rite before no more.

I looked out the glass wall. Clumps of baby green, mauve, and golden buds had painted over treetops. It was pollinating season in New England. On the menu of environmental allergens for me were maple and oak, native to the region. My testing was scheduled at this time so I was exposed to the pollens in the air. If I were allergic to them, my body would exhibit symptoms like swelling, itchiness, rash, fatigue, bloating, and mucus. The more I ingested or got exposed, the less it took to evoke a reaction.

The allergy nurse had marked my arm with a blue pen. I lowered my head to survey the A to E across the top of the arm, and 1 to 6 down its side. So far there were two lines of small raised circles. Some of these bubbles swelled like mosquito bites. I could not scratch them. They had to be measured.

Beep-beep-beep. I poked the buzzer's red stop button and returned to the nurse's station. Vivian, the nurse, superimposed over my arm a thin plastic ruler with circle cutouts to compare the injected sites from three minutes ago. She opened her eyes wide and recorded the radius of each weal.

I sighed and asked, "Am I doing okay?"

"We'll do column C now," she said.

With a gloved hand, Vivian selected a tiny syringe from a white box. Next to it laid a tray of vials containing solutions in various concentrations of allergens. Each cylinder stood like a soldier for inspection.

After inverting a bottle, Vivian sucked out some fluid with the needle. "Here we go."

"Which allergen are you giving me?" I stared at the next space in the grid on my arm. Anxiety turned me into an inquisitive child.

"We'll tell you after this series is done," she said under her glasses.

I better be quiet and sit with my unease.

I got so used to being busy, thinking about what was next on my to-do list that coping with ambiguity called for discipline. My arm was a battlefield of wounds. Some had a red dot where the needle entered, some did not. A thin trace of blood had dried from one injection. Vivian pushed the serum under my skin and discarded the syringe, then reloaded a new one with a different vial. She repeated the process five more times, forming a vertical trail of holes in my arm. She swabbed the area with a cotton ball and handed me the timer. "Come back in three," she smiled and said. I appreciated her gentle yet alert energy, because being needled many times got unnerving.

I padded back to the pink high-back chair in the IV Room. Three lines, eighteen shots in the arm, took forty minutes. The whole test was going to take at least three hours. I began to grasp that in integrative or holistic medicine there were no quick tests or cures. My conventional doctor had given me the radioallergosorbent test, or RAST, which required only one blood draw. It came back negative for all common allergies. The physicians at the Marino Center did not believe the RAST was sensitive enough to measure true allergies.

Here I was getting the skin endpoint titration test, where an increasing amount of allergens were introduced into the body; and after a wait, the size of the skin reaction was assessed. If the skin grew a certain amount, the body had an allergic, or inflammatory, response. Like with the vestibular tests, one had to suffer to get information on the body.

"It's about the load. The body is like a rain barrel," Dr. LaCava had explained two weeks ago. "Chemicals, food, pollen, and mold allergies burden the system. With too many allergens, the barrel spills over. You want to decrease the load by eliminating the allergic substances."

"How does allergy relate to chemical sensitivity?" The rain barrel made sense but I wondered about Dr. LaCava's penchant for tests.

"Those with chemical sensitivity often have allergies," he said. "The immune system is out of sorts. You need to calm it."

I wasn't sure what he meant by calming the immune system. I would like to *be* calm. Needles made me nuts. But like the vitamin C IV, I had no other options, so I scheduled the appointment.

Beep-beep ... I jumped at the sound of the alarm and surveyed the IV patients for signs of disturbance. None.

They were mellow. Some were getting magnesium infusions that relaxed their muscles. I walked to Vivian's desk. My eyelid twitched at the sight of the syringes.

I'll do what it takes. Here goes more pricking.

~

"What do you mean I am allergic to sugar? I have heard of peanut allergies. But sugar?" I spoke with round eyes, a week after the tests.

"Refined white sugar made your body swell, which is an allergic reaction." The nutritionist gazed up from my chart.

That would explain my stuffy ears and sticky eyes in the morning. "But I like sweets." I scanned her empty desk and neat shelves. Her pale face contrasted the black cardigan over black top. No makeup. Deep brown eyes matched her long, narrow Eileen Fisher knit skirt. Her starkness reminded me of a religious statue.

"You can have other sweeteners like honey, maple or rice syrup," she said.

Whew. "And soy? I grew up with soy sauce and tofu. I don't know if I can find foods without soy. It's in everything." I recalled the soy protein bars I ate by the box, thinking it was healthful. "Or corn. I love corn, any form of it," I said.

"If you eat something constantly, the body can get allergic to that. The more you eat it, like the corn, the more you get a high from it. It's like an addiction. When you are addicted to a food, you are probably allergic to it."

I had never heard of this before. I thought that once you found an allergen, you just avoided it. We did that with Noah's allergies. No peanuts, no shellfish. But what was this concept of addiction? Sadly, I resonated with the corn cravings. The daze I got from corn was like a high. Deep down, the corn-induced stupor gave me happiness, of belonging with relatives when I was a child in Taiwan. Corn conjured up Ma's fondness for it, her savory chicken feet corn soup. I had a lot of corn the summer before I got sick with MCS. Did I overload my body's rain barrel?

The list mounted: oats, sugar, corn, soy, oak, maple, dust mites, and maybe wheat. My life continued to mutate into a great unknown.

"No *wheat* pasta," the nutritionist added. "You can have brown rice, millet, buckwheat, quinoa. It's better to avoid the allergens for six months and let your system reset. You can add each food back into your diet, one by one, and watch your reactions."

None of the new items the nutritionist mentioned were in my pantry. "What am I going to eat?" I smirked, as if getting a rise out of this woman was a worthy challenge. I felt deprived and did not like the messenger who took my foods away.

She pulled from a desk drawer a directory of vegetables and their plant families. "You need to consume a variety of protein, veggies, grains, and oils. Rotate your diet. Eat unrelated foods every four days so that the body can process one food in each category and get rid of it."

"You are kidding, right?" I said.

The nutritionist stared.

"Okay. I'll try this rotation diet."

Since my mother moved in with us, she cooked for the household. She would be helpful in the meal preparation. Thank goodness Ma prized wholesome food. Teaching her English names of grains, plants, and oils would be a challenge.

Wait till I tell her she can't use soy sauce anymore.

The nutritionist drew on the cover page of a thick handout on her lap. "Monday, you can have turkey, amaranth, flaxseed oil, cauliflowers, and onions. Shallots are related to onions, so you can use them too. Tuesday, fish, rice, or millet, leeks, spinach, olive oil ..." She listed the grains and plants like she had known them all her life. "Proteins like meat or fish can be interchangeable. They are less of an issue for allergies."

"Oh, good. My mother loves fish. We'll have lots of that," I said.

Thankfully, I liked fish too.

CHAPTER TWELVE

"Aye, no bleach. Strange IV. Now no soy sauce." Ma lamented to the sink and filled a blue tub with water. She passed me on her way to the refrigerator.

"I need to eat differently to get better. It's good for everyone too," I told her. "Today we'll have millet, olive oil, fish, and these vegetables." Pointing at my color-coded sheet on the fridge, I inserted "millet" and "olive oil" in the Taiwanese we speak with each other.

"*Hoh.*" (Okay.) Plastic bags rustled in the veggie bin as my mother made a selection for dinner.

I did not think she listened to me even though she uttered a reply. Despite explanations on MCS, Ma alleged I just needed more sleep and regular hearty meals. I was used to dismissal from others—doctors, friends, but from family, it stung. I wanted my mother on my side, like I had been on hers. I knew the rotation diet was uncommon, inconvenient. I wished I could bypass it and stay unaffected like everyone else, except I couldn't.

    Back at the sink, my mother's petite body slouched over the soaking lettuce.

    "Look at this chart, Ma. Tuesday, blue. Follow the color and cook items in this column. We bought the supplies yesterday." I smoothed over the clear plastic sleeve.

    She rinsed the vegetables and poured out the water.

    "Ma," I said, raising my voice, "would you turn around and see this?"

    "*Un-nah?*" (What?) She cranked her neck. Through her glasses, the bottom half of her eyes appeared bigger than the top half.

    "Please cook millet for dinner. Millet," I repeated.

    "How I cook mee-let?" Her hands were pink from cold water.

    "Mil-let. Come look at this sheet and you will know how it's spelled."

    "Ah-yah. My hand wet. You bring mee-let." She extracted dark red and green lettuce and loaded the salad spinner.

    Giving up on the menu chart, I went across the floor and grabbed the grain from the pantry. I put the bag on the counter next to my mother. "The cooking instructions are here." I tapped the back of the glossy package.

My mother yanked the salad spinner's string, let it recoil, and repeated the tug-of-war. *Whoosh. Whoosh.* Exhausted from a long workday, I felt my head start to whirl with the contraption.

"Ma." I brought the millet in front of her face. "Read how to cook here. Okay?" *Please just take over.* I wanted to change from work clothes and check on Noah.

The salad spinner came to a stop. Ma looked up at the tiny round seeds. "You help cook mee-let first time. I no read instruction. You tell me."

"You can read it." I knew she could. She had done okay with her English for twenty years.

"I no cook mee-let." She pulled hard at the salad spinner again. The leaves flew to the walls of the tub.

I retreated and glared at my mother's back.

She said she came to help me ...

"You always say you don't know how and I end up doing it!" I slammed the millet on the counter.

"*Herh-la. Herh-la.*" (Okay. Okay.) She walked away.

I rushed to my study and stripped off my clothes. My pulse thundered as I threw on sweats and a mismatched top. I had screamed at my seemingly gentle mother. Outside the window, trees lined the cul-de-sac and cars dotted driveways. Across the street the two-story house remained. All was intact.

Ma had done a lot for us. How could I be enraged by her simple request? I collapsed in my chair. A tiny fuse lit a big bomb. Especially when the fuse got shortened by a chronic illness. My mother's helplessness, directives, and expectations, no matter the size, weighed on me since I existed. As the eldest, I was practically born an adult. I was potty trained at one. Ma raised me to "know light and heavy" by anticipating and addressing others' needs. The child served the parent without being asked. When I learned English, I became Ma's translator and default front person. Add this to her claim that she stayed in a bad marriage for her kids, I was forever obligated.

Perhaps I wanted to rescue myself by saving Ma. I grew up watching my father oppress her, knowing that my existence caused her to endure so much. The guilt made me a vessel for her complaints, my father's wrath, and the fallout from their fights. My mother's trouble was mine. Last year, pre-MCS, I rallied to help her end the marriage. During the divorce both my parents called me to unload their grievances. The process broke me—my fantasy of having a decent childhood dissolved.

I loved my mother. I wrote my college application essay about her, the person I admired most. She was the seventh girl among twelve siblings. Her parents got tired of naming one more daughter so they ask the city registry to give her a name. The registry named her Snow. She was born in January, also with a father who hit, and before school she salvaged cabbage leaves behind vendors at the day market to feed the pigs at home. She persevered, always with a purpose. A diehard caretaker, Ma used to warm our clothes between her sweater and belly while we bathed in unheated, forty-degree Fahrenheit Taiwanese winters. After losing Jonah, I entrusted Noah only to Ma. When we needed a babysitter, which was twice in Noah's life, my mother drove from New York to watch him.

Was it a good idea to have Ma living with us? Roger and I invited my mother to move in so she would feel safe about leaving my father. We bought our current house with her in mind. She did not want to impose and needed a reason to move in. I promptly gave her one when my body went haywire after the vein surgery.

Now the ghost of our past lurked in the daily routines. I had forgotten this was the woman who wept, "When will you be normal?" when she dropped me off at the train station. I was twenty-one, in a miniskirt en route to a party. I was never a demure, proper Taiwanese daughter as my name Sue-Yi implied. I had failed to fit Ma's mold. She was the dissatisfied custodian, I the angry emotional keeper. I did not think of this when I beckoned her to live with us. My mother, with her graying hair and shrinking stature, still commanded my calm in a flash. Her dismay overwhelmed. I felt I had to take care of her above all else.

Today I wanted to get off that treadmill.

Twilight painted the sky a copper hue and cast dark shapes on the floor. I needed to find Noah. I went through the kitchen to the TV room. My son hovered over a laptop next to wall-length sliders. Four huge trunks of oak and a wall of blueberry bushes were fading into shadows. Noah perched over a child-size table and chair. His thumb clicked as fast as his index finger glided over the touchpad.

"How was school today?" I rubbed his head.

"Good."

"Did you do the counting beads?" Noah's teachers reported he strung beads to learn multiplication at lightning speed. He was up to the number eight. I lowered my head next to his. A bowl of cubed, peeled apple sat next to the computer. My son's eyes were transfixed by its screen. "Did you hear me?" I said.

No answer.

"What are you making?"

"A sign-up sheet."

"That's neat. What are you making it for?"

Index finger continued to work the touchpad.

"Why aren't you answering me?" I boomed.

He jerked in his chair. Finally, I had an effect on *someone*.

"What, Mommy?" His big brown eyes waited.

I went blank. "Eat your apples. *Amah* (maternal grandma) made them for you."

Next door in the kitchen, my mother called. "*Lye-la, lye-la!*" (Come here!) "Help me cook this."

Surely she heard me yelling at Noah. My father had scolded me when he was displeased. Had I become him?

This was not the first time I mistook my child for a release valve. And because of Noah's advanced skills, I forgot he was five.

Massaging my forehead, I went to the sack of millet in the kitchen and read the instructions. "You put two and a half cups of water in with a cup of grain." I found the measuring cup in the cupboard. "Add salt and olive oil in the pot to boil."

"Instruction no say add oil," Ma corrected me.

So she could read the directions.

I waved my hand. "I know, but it might make it taste better. You can change things a little. Follow the color in the chart. Don't mix up the foods in the chart from day to day."

"*Hoh*." She placed the ingredients in a stainless pot and placed a lid on it.

"Are we having haddock today?" We lived on an island when I was a child, and one rare thing my parents shared was the worship of fresh seafood. I turned to the wooden cutting board on the kitchen peninsula. A slab of white fish with pinkish veins waited to be cut. Ma had defrosted it by leaving the wrapped parcel in a Styrofoam tray overnight.

My mother nodded. "Very frosh (fresh), right?" My mother would drive miles to get fresh seafood or corn. "Fry it with garlic?"

"No, according to the blue column in the chart, today we use leeks."

"Leek. *Hoh.*"

"*Sieh-sieh.*" (Thank you.) I glanced at my mother's face. Not quite an apology, but it was sincere.

"No need to thank." Her eyes fixed on the pot on the stove.

It was too easy to take family members for granted. We were accessible and it was assumed we would bless each other with unconditional love. Ma and I were the water boiling in the pot, trying to meld to make millet. Maybe this was why we lived together again—to excavate the old dynamics and transmute them.

~

It was my turn to help Noah to bed. I pulled down the shade in his room to block the beam from a streetlight and turned on the lamp on the nightstand. I patted the bed. "Hey, climb in."

Noah, whose body dangled inside an adult-size T-shirt, inserted himself between the fluffy-clouds-on-blue-sky sheets. I pulled the comforter over his chest and sat next to him. I read *The Story of Cars* while he relished vibrant drawings in the paperback. Warmth radiated from his small frame along my leg.

"Mommy, can you tell Amah not to give me big pieces of apple?"

"Apples are good for you. She worries about you not eating vegetables so she's pushing fruit."

"I want small pieces of apple. You used to make 'book apples.'" I cut the fruit into thin rectangular slices. Noah likened them to books.

"I'll tell Amah. Do you like her being here?"

"Yes. She always picks me up on time."

"That's good, buddy. That way I don't have to rush from work like a mad woman on the highway."

We finished the book. I put it on the nightstand. "Sing, Mommy. Sing." He reached out for my hand. The tenderness from his soft palm conveyed lovingkindness. *Only peace to you, Noah. Only peace.*

I did the usual repertoire, "Sing a Song of Sixpence a Pocket Full of Rye," "Twinkle, Twinkle Little Star," and a Taiwanese lullaby:

> *Rock baby-ah, Rock baby-ah*
> *Rock baby-ah, go to sleep*
> *Rock baby-ah, Rock baby-ah.*
> *Wish you real good sleep*
> *Our child is so adorable*
> *Face is so gorgeous.*

My mother's eldest sister, whom I called *Dua-Yi* and with whom we lived when I was young, taught Ma this song. She passed it on to me when Noah was born.

My elders imparted something good—this was a revelation, as I had mistrusted the culture that sanctioned the abuse of women and children. Here was a serenade, a way to love my son. It worked every time. His grip loosened. I gazed at his closed eyes and long lashes, wondering how I could have been so cross. I was grateful he still wanted to hold my hand and hear me sing.

CHAPTER THIRTEEN

Sitting between a big window and a desk in the Marino Center office, Dr. LaCava extracted two pieces of paper from a folder and handed me one. "We tested for heavy metals. The arsenic and lead levels look fine."

I was glad we had ripped out the pressure-treated wood in the storage room.

"But the mercury level is extremely high," he added.

I stared at my report. On a color continuum where green was "low" and red was "high," the dot indicating my blood mercury level surpassed the "high" marker. It almost fell off the line.

"What does this mean?" My legs sweat on the coarse fabric seat.

"It means you *are* exposed to mercury constantly."

"I have a whole mouthful of silver fillings. Could that be it?"

"No, the elemental mercury from fillings usually gets lodged in your brain, organs, and accumulates over time. That's not good either, but it doesn't appear in the blood. If it's in your blood, it's in your environment. Your whole family should be tested."

Oh my. My heart sank to my stomach.

Noah.

The timing was bad. I woke up this morning with the room spinning. It was the onset of my period and the MCS often worsened during this time of the month. Dr. LaCava had me track my cycles and basal body temperature. On top of everything else, he was looking for thyroid problems.

The sunlight behind him was glaring. "Say that again? Mercury is in my house?"

"It may be."

"Is mercury the cause of chemical sensitivity?"

"It could be. Remember the rain barrel. We try to decrease the load on the body."

I wanted to lunge over the desk and shake him for clear answers, not "could be," "maybe." It had been seven months since I began with Dr. LaCava. Even though he was the only one who seemed to have methods to uncover something about the MCS and his treatments had started to help with the load on my body—my eyes ceased to be sticky after the rotation diet and I had more energy—I wanted a concrete explanation.

What do I have to do to get well? my brain shouted. But I grinned. I would finish with dignity, rage later. "Good that we found out," I said. Having a high concentration of toxic metal in my blood made me feel defective. I sleepwalked out of the meeting. The noisy street added to my agitation.

"Guess what LaCava found this time?" I said into the cell phone while walking to my car.

"More rusting in your body?" Roger said, half-jokingly.

"No-oh. Mercury in the blood."

"Mercury?"

"Strange, isn't it? I'm exposed to it somehow. He said the entire household should get checked ... I'm worried about Noah."

"Sounds bad, but let's get him tested first."

I got into the Volvo. Through the windshield, the contrast between the azure sky and verdant trees annoyed me. It was wasted on bad news.

~

After arguing with Noah's pediatrician to administer the blood test prescribed by Dr. LaCava, we were relieved to learn that Noah's mercury level registered in the low range. It was considered "normal" given the pollutants in the world. Roger's mercury level was high—but not off the chart like mine. Ma declined the workup because her insurance would not cover it and she did not think it was a big deal.

On the July Fourth weekend, Roger rented a Jerome Mercury Vapor Analyzer from a local environmental health store. It was used to check air quality after a mercury spill.

"How does this work?" I asked, grateful that Roger was an engineer at heart and loved gadgets.

He put the meter on a crate in his office. On its top, a screen and handle extended over an indent in the middle of the device. Roger pointed at the black probe at the end of the rectangular metal box the size of a loaf of bread. "You stick this into wherever after you calibrate it."

"I hope we can find the source of the mercury. It doesn't make sense that you and I have a high level and Noah doesn't," I said.

"He doesn't have any metal fillings in his teeth. You think that's it?"

"Dr. LaCava doesn't think fillings would cause a high level of mercury in the blood. But I wonder if the stuff in our mouth would register on this meter." I had read that mercury vapor escaped from fillings when disturbed. The website of the International Academy of Oral Medicine and Toxicology showed a picture of the noxious substance spiraling away from a filled molar.

We taped a paper towel over the probe. Not the most scientific method, but enough to start an experiment. Roger, whose mouth was graced by sixteen silver amalgams, put his lips over the paper towel, and nothing registered. He brushed his teeth and bent over to the receptacle. A beep and a red 15 appeared on the screen, meaning the device detected 15 micrograms of mercury vapor per liter of air. The E.P.A. and U.S. Department of Health and Human Services, in its 2012 report on mercury cleanup policy recommendations, cited 10 micrograms per liter as the level at which residents should evacuate in a spill.

Continuing with our investigation, Roger fetched a bowl of pretzels from the kitchen. He crunched some, put his mouth over the meter, and got a reading of 25.

"Geez. How much of this stuff are we eating and inhaling?" I gasped.

"I'm not sure, but it can't be good."

"How come you are not sick and I am?"

"I don't know, Sue-Yi." I loved it when he called me by my given name. "Maybe some people are more sensitive."

Like Jeff May, I was the canary in the mine in our family. Roger changed the paper towel on the tip of the meter. I brushed my teeth, put my mouth over the meter, and got similar results.

My body was a toxic soup. Even if mercury fillings were not associated with blood contamination, having them in my mouth felt wrong. Not helping my body's rain barrel.

We were onto something in the mouth. But Dr. LaCava's charge was to find the heavy metal in our surroundings. I suggested we check my office at Cheever House next.

~

A beautiful destination for work, Cheever House's dark brown roof and chimneys imposed over three stories of windows and cream sidings. Flanked by acres of green, the estate, once someone's home, was donated to Wellesley College and divided into over thirty offices. On the holiday weekend, the parking lot was empty. We drove to the front entrance as if we lived there. In the afternoon, sheep baaed from an adjacent farm. I unlocked the heavy wooden door and met cool mustiness from the dark front hall.

We ascended the wide, winding mahogany stairs under a chandelier. My office, which I shared with two other women, was near the top of the building. Its oppressive air and piercing sun from the giant windows assaulted us as I opened the door. My barrel-like air cleaner hummed in the room. It was my insurance against allergens and was left running at all times. I had meetings here wearing a canister gas mask to avoid inhaling ink fumes from printouts. It startled my colleagues at first.

"It's a steam room," Roger said. He turned on the Jerome meter and crawled under the desks.

"Sorry, no central air." I followed him, eyes peeled on the digital screen. We went around four dusty tables and two rows of tall metal file cabinets.

"Nothing," Roger reported. He stood up, sweat trickling from his shiny forehead.

"Let's check the bathroom, down the hall on the left." In my mind I traced the rooms I used while at work.

On the restroom walls, posters urging kids to read reflected one of my boss's research interests. The floor had a few bottles of cleaners, which made me dizzy. I opened the window next to the toilet, and Roger surveyed the perimeter with the instrument.

"Anything?" I leaned against the window. My hope to find the culprit began to wane.

"Nope." Roger wiped his face with a paper towel from a dispenser.

"Glad we checked it out. I thought this old place would be likely to have mercury."

"How about the conference room?" Roger asked. I followed him as he headed toward the stairs.

On the main level, a library lined with carved panels and books doubled as a meeting space. Roger crouched under chairs and a massive wooden table. Perspiration left a big black stain on his gray T-shirt.

He stood up. "Nothing. Back to the drawing board."

"That's disappointing."

"Better that you don't find anything."

I sighed. "Sorry for the wild goose chase, Rog. Thanks for coming."

We exited Cheever House with the meter in a tote bag.

Back at home, Roger pointed the machine in every corner. Zilch. I fretted that we were being exposed to a poison we could not find. At the end of the long weekend, he tried again. In the kitchen, Roger opened each cabinet under the sink. The meter beeped when he got to the third one.

"Hey, I got a 6 here," he yelled behind the kitchen peninsula.

I ran toward his kneeling body. "What's causing it?"

"I don't know."

He reached into the cabinet and pulled out a tall trash bin, a plastic basket with new sponges, and a bottle of natural cleaning spray. He poked the instrument into the cupboard. "Hmm ... now there isn't any reading."

He put everything back.

"Now there's the 6 again. Weird," he said, shaking his head.

Goosebumps popped up all over my body. Roger held the probe over the white garbage can.

"It says 9. Is this thing empty? Looks it." He tilted the deep container.

"I think so." I had just changed the bag that evening. Thanks to the vitamin C IV and a new diet, I could tolerate plastic again.

"Let's see ..." He turned his wrist and oriented the meter toward the bottom. "Wow—it says 150." Roger reached in and pulled out a small package in two layers of plastic. "What is this?"

"I don't know. My mother's handiwork. She was working here earlier."

Roger untied the outer bag and stuck the tip of the Jerome meter in it. A loud beep zapped the air. It displayed 650 in bright red letters. "Wow! What's in here?"

I flew downstairs to my mother's room and found her watching the Yankees.

"Ma. MA!" My brows arched from seeing the red 6-5-0. "What was in that little bag in the trash can?" I called.

"Why? It smell? I double-bag," she said.

"No, it doesn't smell. What was in it?"

"Sardine. I clean fish. Very frosh."

"Ma, the meter we rented? It found a lot of mercury in that bag."

As part of my rotation diet, and to my mother's delight, we ate fish almost every day. It was nutritious, heart-healthy, the best. Ma selected all our fish at the seafood counter. We liked sardines because it was low on the food chain and supposedly had less mercury than its marine predators. Noah was a picky eater who occasionally had fish. He was spared the high amount of mercury.

"*Black-white speak!* (Nonsense!) Fish good food!" Ma's eyes nailed me.

"I don't know anymore, Ma." I sprinted back upstairs.

"Rog, sardines! Sardines were in the bag."

"The amount of mercury blew out the device. I need to reset it." Sitting on the floor, Roger stared at the sack of fish parts, then the fried Jerome meter. "Unbelievable. How could fish have so much mercury? This is way more than just breaking a thermometer," he said. "Mercury is toxic. I don't want it in my mouth."

I had told Roger about a clinic in Montreal, Canada, I had heard about at the Marino Center. Hal Huggins, an American dentist and one of the first to speak against mercury amalgams, supervised dental revisions there. He taught detoxing classes for the chemically and immune challenged.

"I'll go to the program in Montreal with you," he said, knowing it would take a week and over ten thousand dollar per person, depending on the dental work needed.

"I'm so glad!" I had tried to convince Roger that a whole mouthful of amalgams was bad, even if he was not sick. "I'm sorry it'll cost a lot, but our health is worth it."

Although Dr. LaCava said dental mercury would not appear in blood, getting readings from chewing, brushing our teeth, and from the food we ate were sufficient for us to spring for the dental detox program.

"We're burning through our savings. We can't fix the house or add the patio we want in the backyard. I'm still cranking up a practice. But we'll make the money back somehow." Roger shrugged.

"I just want the junk out of my body. I don't care about a patio," I sat next to him and reached for his hand.

"What about the fish?"

"Wait till I tell Dr. LaCava."

It would be hard to eat fish ever again.

CHAPTER FOURTEEN

"This says if you want to sue me, you will do it in Canada." The anesthesiologist with a French accent handed me a clipboard. "Please sign before we begin."

In a dentist's chair, groggy from waking up at dawn and stomach growling, I took the pen from his hand and paused. I came to clean up my mouth and get rid of MCS. *If I consider suing, I might as well go home now.* I signed in my typical illegible movie star manner.

Manon, one of three assistants in the clinic, pulled on blue rubber gloves. Her auburn hair shined against the mint green walls. "How are you?" she asked me.

"Feels like being in the electric chair waiting for execution."

"Don't worry. We'll take good care of you. You won't get sick as long as you don't swallow blood."

A childhood memory of being fed congealed pig blood burst in my mouth. I gulped down the iron-tinged disgust.

"The paper I signed said that I could die from anesthesia. But I am sure I'll be fine," I said to Manon. The program's brochure and my research indicated that conscious sedation for the dental work I was about to have was tolerable for the chemically sensitive. I hoped I would not end up as sick as I was after the vein surgery.

"Good morning. Today's your day and tomorrow is Roger's." The owner of the practice, Dr. Benoit, took a long stride into the room and shook my hand. His green eyes and easy smile melted my worries. He gestured to someone in a white coat behind him and introduced a doctor with a French name I could not remember. "He will work on your teeth too-day. I'll stop in periodically."

I did not expect someone else to work on my mouth. Yesterday I met with Dr. Benoit to discuss the "job": Replace fourteen mercury amalgams and one nickel crown, remove a newly found impacted fifth wisdom tooth, and clean out four in-gum, bacteria-filled cavitations from previous extractions.

Dr. So-and-So better be great.

He was an unknown, entrusted with thousands of dollars of dental work and my health. Going with whatever the doctors wanted did not work well before. But we had come this far. I leaned back to let the anesthesiologist survey my arms for veins. With pre-op tests, travel, and child care arrangements, I forgot to worry about the IV sedation. My blood vessels were thinned by twelve hours of fasting. The anesthesiologist spoke to Manon while holding up two index fingers an inch apart. She nodded and pressed her fingers over a segment on my wrist. The needle was threaded quickly and an IV was connected. In an instant my brain felt like a big wad of tissue.

"We are going to freeze you," someone said.

What natural numbing method had they invented in Canadian biological dentistry? I was glad not to have shots. But then a large syringe came toward my mouth. Freezing meant Novocain. The needle stung the inside of my cheek. My head fell back in total relaxation and the jaw opened to receive several gloved hands. After a while someone would return my mouth to a closed position. I floated in a mint-green fog as drills pounced and picks scraped my teeth. These noises landed at the edge of my mind. Beyond that there was nothing. At times cotton rolls were stuffed in the back of my mouth like I was the Thanksgiving turkey.

A break was announced and I went to the restroom with the IV pole. I had some faculties left—the conscious part of the sedation. Manon assisted me. After that, more freezing and drilling, opening and shutting. I thought of snapping turtles.

"We are finished," Manon declared.

The IV left my aching wrist, and the back of my chair was raised. A warm sickness in my stomach exploded.

Manon grabbed a metal trash can and held it under my chin. "You must have swallowed blood!"

I whipped forward and hurled. Supposedly the conscious sedation was okay for people like me? Fear and doubt, like the vomit, appeared as soon as I got rid of it. Someone's fingers pressed my shoulders and neck. Lymphatic massage was a part of the program to aid drainage of toxins released from the procedure. It was not helping fast enough.

I drank my own blood. I leaned in the trash can. The fingers on my shoulders came with me.

An hour later, Dr. Benoit appeared. "Are you feeling better?" He spoke to Manon in French and she left the room.

"After throwing up, much better," I said, dry heaving.

Manon returned with a box of ginger tea. Its cellophane wrapping crunched in her hand. Dr. Benoit gave me the tea. "Drink this for nausea. Rest tomorrow and call us if needed. You were in the chair for seven hours."

Seven hours? Plus an hour of puking. That was a whole day's work. "Glad it's over. Thank you," I mumbled with a numb face.

The dentist patted my shoulder and left.

"How're you doing?" Roger said softly as he emerged in the doorway.

"I drank blood. Must have been gallons because I threw up for an hour."

"I heard from next door."

We sat in the reception area and I rested my head on his shoulder. The image of my vomiting into the garbage can replayed in my head. Twenty minutes later, Roger squeezed my hand. "The color is coming back to your face. Time to go?"

"Let's blow this joint." I stood up. Like a tornado, the nausea came and went. Some wooziness lingered. We bid the receptionist farewell and descended the stone steps outside. At the bottom of the stairs, I turned to take in the exterior of the clinic. The brownstone's climbing vines, and laughter from kids playing nearby told me I had returned to the human world.

~

Two days later, at our hotel in Montreal, Ma followed Dr. Huggins's recipe and liquefied organic beef and avocado with a blender we brought from home. It was to replenish blood and protein lost in the dental surgery. With salt, the goop tasted scrumptious.

"Big cheeks make you two look nice," Ma insisted with a grin. "You both too skinny."

"Ma, you are crazy." I stared at the mirror in the kitchenette. Chipmunk cheeks accentuating an already round countenance. I had achieved what the Taiwanese called "meat patty face."

"Today we have a class with Dr. Huggins," I said to Roger, who stood next to me in the reflection. "You get to try the miraculous vitamin C."

"Should be fun."

"Yeah. You weren't sick to begin with," I said. Roger called his six hours in the chair "the best nap I've ever had." The lymphatic masseuse mentioned that Roger's systems drained extremely well. I was glad for him, and relieved to know that a professional could tell the difference between our bodies, as MCS seemed invisible.

We hugged Ma and Noah and headed toward the elevator.

"Puking aside, I'm not as sick as I might have been after being sedated for hours. Just a little off." I reached for Roger's hand.

"That's good," he said with a smile.

"I must be stronger now." I pumped a fist. "Let's hope this dental revision got rid of the chemical sensitivity."

Roger kissed my moon face.

We walked four long blocks to another hotel downtown, where Dr. Huggins taught classes on detoxing and blood chemistry. On a crisp July morning, people in T-shirts and shorts sauntered on sidewalks and clustered in cafes. Signs in French and English dotted the street. The hum of traffic blended with Roger's and my discussion on whether Hal Huggins was a pioneer or a charlatan. For decades he campaigned against mercury dental materials, earning him notoriety. He claimed his methodology of detoxing cured himself of multiple sclerosis. I looked forward to hearing about his work.

~

"Slap my hand!" In the hotel classroom, I encouraged the plain-clothed nurse. "Whatever you do, I hope you get a vein." My body yearned for a massive dose of vitamin C.

Lucy flexed my arm toward her and pressed her lips together. She was to hook up ten participants to the antioxidant while Dr. Huggins lectured.

"In the next two days," he began, "you will learn about eating clean and balancing your blood chemistry. You'll understand dental and mercury toxicity and how to recover." Dr. Huggins paced near the projection screen in front of us. "Let's start. Guess what kind of car I inherited from my father when he died?" His grin revealed two large front teeth. His blue eyes twinkled.

"A BMW?" someone called out.

"A Cadillac?" said another.

Dr. Huggins shook his head.

"A Mercury!"

We giggled like school children. Around the oblong table, people listened over pens and papers. We got acquainted by our diseases and hometowns: multiple sclerosis, Atlanta, Buffalo, New York; hepatitis C, Houston; chemical sensitivity, Boston; chronic fatigue, Toronto.

Lucy tightened the tourniquet above my right elbow. My arm bloated with hints of blue.

"Here's how the body deals with chemicals we put in it every day." Dr. Huggins's high and low tones added irony. "How many of you drink coffee regularly?"

I scanned the room as the nurse swabbed me. Six hands went up. Not me. I loved the aroma but not the racing heart I got from the drink.

"I'm going to play a video on the effect of caffeine." The gray projection screen brightened. The William Tell Overture accompanied a woman drinking from a mug. Dr. Huggins narrated, "This drink is going through the digestive system ..."

The nurse pierced my skin with a shiny needle. As expected, she grazed under the skin for a vein. And as expected, she could not find one.

Drops of sweat rolled from Lucy's silver-gray scalp. She tried another site.

"Caffeine reaches the liver ..." The doc explained the biochemical process involved. "Now to the kidney ... the bladder ..."

The woman on the screen ran to a bathroom and slammed its door.

"Isn't the body exhausted by now?" the video concluded.

A few chuckles peppered the room. At my seat, anxiety fused Lucy and me. She prevailed on the fourth try.

"Thank you!" I exclaimed, my voice louder than the presentation. I ducked with embarrassment. The others smiled at me. Camaraderie of the chronically ill. I got it in the IV Room at the Marino Center too.

The nurse went to the pale hepatitis C patient from Houston. I settled in my chair and perused the content of the tote bag we received. Imprinted on it was a dragon's head inside a red shield. The same shield and I AM A DRAGON SLAYER was watermarked on a pad of paper. I was there to kill MCS.

"Lucy?" I raised my free hand after ten minutes.

She came toward me from a seat next to the wall.

"What's the concentration of C in this solution?" I asked.

"Thirty grams."

"I'm used to twenty. It's stinging. Could you slow it down?"

Lucy rolled the switch on the IV line. "Better?"

I nodded.

The lecture went on to the usage of clear glass and cast iron cookware, the only materials that do not release harmful chemicals or metals in high heat. On the subject of seafood, Dr. Huggins confirmed Roger's and my suspicions with his graduate study in toxicology. Humans had polluted so much, oceans were connected, and all fish had become filters for PCBs and heavy metals like mercury. It resonated. We had seen sardine remains setting off the Jerome meter.

Wrapped in a cocoon of dim air conditioning, I questioned reality. Coffee, seafood, and mercury fillings could wreak havoc in the body to the level of toxicity, yet politicians and doctors deemed them safe. In a pure state, omega-3s from fish were beneficial to our health, but when the source was contaminated—where do we draw the line? Was there such a thing as a *benign* level of a toxin? If mercury was harmful to children and pregnant women, why was it okay for other people? What were we being told, and not told?

I stared at the tall, slender Hal Huggins. Before coming to Montreal, I discovered reports online accusing him of quackery. I also learned he had been skewered by the American Dental Association. Roger's family had grilled us on the validity of dental detoxing. Despite the controversy surrounding Huggins and his therapies, what he presented here made sense. Conventional medicine failed to identify or treat the MCS. It even exacerbated the condition by way of anti-nausea medication, general anesthesia, and pills. There was no reason for me to cling to the established view of health care. I would give the "quack" a chance.

My arm ached until the nurse slowed the IV way down.

"This bottle will finish at five o'clock if you want all of it," she said.

I do, after four sticks. "Everyone will be done at noon. I'll be here without lunch," I whined to Roger, who sat next to me.

"I'll bring you a sandwich," he said.

When my IV ended, the room cheered. My wooziness from the dental surgery was gone too.

We spent another day with Dr. Huggins. He covered ancestral diets, complete blood count reports, the ideal numbers for cholesterol, hematocrit, white blood cells, and more. I was inspired by his fight for his health and hoped the MCS was gone.

~

"Noah! It's lovely," I squealed under the sun.

On our last day in Montreal, we visited the Mosaiculture Internacionales Festival 2003 at the Old Port. In the competition, thirty-two countries submitted elaborately decorated scenes made from plant cuttings, depicting legends of the world: a phoenix rising, a flying carpet, Moby Dick, the Great Wall ... Panels of blossoms and sprigs living in small tubes of liquid made up the intricate displays.

"It's too bright," Noah said, squinting. "Can you carry me?"

"No, walking is a good change from watching TV for a week." I rubbed his head.

My nose picked up the odor of chemical fertilizer, which I recognized from being in gardening stores. I searched around me. Only greenness, my shadow, and Noah. "Look at the gigantic statues. This is Easter Island. That's Buddha." I pointed.

"Can you carry me?" At five and skinny, Noah sometimes got his way.

"No, buddy. You need the walk."

My mother slowed down to take Noah's hand.

I caught up to Roger, who stood in front of Quebec's entry, *Mother Earth*, a huge woman's head made from clusters of emerald, baby green leaves, red and magenta flowers. Her closed eyes sat above a serene smile. Plush shapes of open-winged ducks flocked toward her from the glassy water. From two high, outstretched hands, voluminous streams of water gushed between verdant fingers. My eyes welled up. This was magical, sacred. What luck for me to be here during this festival. And to complete the dental revision and have my family with me. I etched *Mother Earth* on my brain.

"Aye." Lightheaded, I sat at a nearby bench and closed my eyes.

Roger came toward me.

"I thought you were okay being outside?"

"Me too. They must use a lot of chemicals to keep the plants fresh for the weeklong festival. I smell them."

MCS was the shadow that followed me.

"You are doing okay." Roger roped his arm around my shoulder.

"After all this work, cost, and dragging everyone here. I'm sorry." Tears covered my face. "Damn this body. I want to be free, free of it!"

"It's all you've got. We just gutted our mouths and we'll eat better. We are going in the right direction."

I lifted my head and gazed at the artificially preserved *Mother Earth*. The water continued to flow from her hands.

CHAPTER FIFTEEN

Two small bottles of herbal extracts stood next to the computer in Dr. Gordin's office. The holistic doctor at the Marino Center and I were surrounded by succulent plants in the afternoon light. A bushy mustache dominated Dr. Gordin's face. It reminded me of a giant caterpillar.

"How can I feel normal again?" My anxiety uncorked at the centipede.

"Normal?"

"Recently I came back from Hal Huggins's dental clinic," I said. "I thought I'd feel much better right away, but I didn't. I see Dr. LaCava for chemical sensitivity, someone else for more testing, and people in the IV Room suggest that I see you too."

Sheepish about collecting doctors, I also felt oddly accomplished. Maybe this man would be the beacon in my quest for health. Dr. LaCava was losing me with his new enthusiasm for hydrogen peroxide IVs—a potent detoxing agent but badly stung my veins.

"Hal Huggins. Wow." Dr. Gordin's face lit up. "How was that?" His thick Russian accent gave a sense of kinship, that we were both foreign born.

"Eye opening and challenging." I recounted the detox program and went back to the onset of the chemical sensitivity a year and a half ago.

"I'm tired and push myself to do things. I hold my breath pumping gas and watch what I eat because of food allergies. Dr. Huggins says to eat nothing from the ocean or pigs. But I grew up eating pork and fish—"

"Does the vitamin C IV help?" Dr. Gordin cupped his chin and perused his computer monitor.

"Yes. I have more energy after the IVs. It got rid of nausea from the sedation in Montreal."

"Then keep doing it." He glanced at my file. "I see in your records you have done many tests at the Marino Center."

"Yes. I even have an ID card that says formaldehyde and benzene are major irritants for me."

Dr. Gordin pulled out a pad. "Tell me about yourself."

Really? I had a lot to say. I described part-time research job and career counseling background, my intelligent five-year-old, my dedicated but needy mother, and my stressed-out, kind husband. Under framed diplomas and certificates from Leningrad and Chicago, Dr. Gordin filled up one page and flipped over the paper.

"How well do you sleep?" He bowed his head as he wrote.

Why did that matter? "I sleep badly. Nightmares all the time. I often wake up exhausted with my stomach in a knot."

"That's horrible. When you say 'all the time,' how long has it been? A week? A month? A year? All your life?"

"All my life," I chirped, as if I'd won a title. "Growing up, my parents fought a lot. Usually after we went to bed. They didn't talk to each other unless they had to."

I forgot something.

"Oh ... and I lost a newborn in 1996. Jonah stopped breathing within the hour he was born. I thought he was sleeping while he was latched onto the breast. He was a full-term healthy baby."

Dr. Gordin frowned.

"Forceps, according to an expert witness," I added. "There is a lawsuit going on." Sadness rushed to my eyes. "We took him off the ventilator on his fourth day."

"I am so sorry to hear that. So sorry." The doctor shook his head. His brown eyes radiated concern. "Wow." He sighed. And paused.

"Thank you." I gazed at him. "I never slept well when the next baby came. He coughed, I woke up. I listened for him to stir." Looking away to hide my tears, I turned on my game face. "Everyone's got something. Five years after

Jonah, I helped my mother with her divorce. Then I got sick."

Half an hour passed. I thought I should stop talking. But Dr. Gordin waited patiently as I brought him up to date.

"I did vestibular testing, moved out of our house, moved back, had vein surgery, dental revision ... I haven't been able to shake the MCS even though I'm doing all this stuff to get better."

"I see. Your body needs rest."

Rest was the last word I expected to hear.

Dr. Gordin nodded as he spread out his palms. "If the brain doesn't stop telling the body to fight or flight, like in PTSD, the body cannot sleep. You need to REALLY rest so the body can replenish itself. Do you read before bedtime?" His eyes fixed on mine.

I nodded.

"What do you read?"

"Murder mysteries." I was an Agatha Christie fan.

"No, no. You need to read something calming. Me-ta-physical."

"Meta" always confused me. I searched my head. "Like the *Seat of the Soul?*"

"Absolutely."

"That would make me sleepy." I read half of it last fall and could not finish.

"What do you do for re-lac-sation?" His caterpillar danced with each syllable. "Do you meditate?"

"I jog twice a week, a mile and a half." It was an accomplishment since the illness. "I think of nothing during a jog. Does that count?"

Dr. Gordin shook his head and leaned forward. "Do you do yoga? Qigong? Tai chi?"

Face flushed, I confessed no, despite the fact that my heritage produced two of the three techniques. "I sit in a sauna to sweat toxins?" I was not used to getting a doctor's disapproval. "What does relaxation have to do with chemical sensitivity?"

"Your brain is on hypervigilance. It is on guard all the time. Your sympathetic nervous system is on alert, sending out stress hormones." He put two palms together and nodded toward me, his eyes eager. "The brain wants to attack everything—food, chemicals, everything. It is kicking everything out of the body."

"Plato said the part cannot be well unless the whole is well," he continued. We need to examine the *overall aspect* of your health so you can recover. The overall aspect." The doctor's voice reached a crescendo. "You need to calm down the brain." He motioned with his left hand as if he was introducing the organ on his desk.

I wanted to respond to the passionate plea with as much enthusiasm. But the charge to relax overwhelmed me. It was *more* to do. "I could ... I could do tai chi. I have a video tape at home I could try." I bought it years ago and it was still in shrink-wrap.

"Good. Try tai chi, keep up the IVs. Come back to see me in a month." He printed out a referral sheet and handed it to me. "And see the nutritionist for a hypoglycemic diet. You mentioned that you get dizzy when you're hungry."

I left Dr. Gordin's office and checked the clock in the hallway. He spent an hour with me and took four pages of notes. My chest was a yin-yang mixture of sunshine and mud. I ran down the stairs and got into my car. Half an hour later I was inside the shiny green fences of Westview Cemetery. I parked on a curve near the entrance and hurried to a plaque six rows in, next to a young Japanese maple.

Kneeling over the salmon-pink granite, I pushed the grass and dirt away from its beveled edges. The soft wet soil smudged my fingertips. Why did the grass grow so quickly? My tears dotted the stone. It read:

Jonah Chen Glovsky
December 16–20, 1996
Our First Love

I rubbed my hand over the indent of Jonah's name. Pounding the stone, I whispered: "Jonah, somebody listened for a long time and understood. He said he was sorry to hear about what happened to you. He was truly sorry. He felt deeper than any doctor who knew about you."

A doctor, a stranger, a man acknowledged my son and was moved by his story. He wanted to know how I ended up this way. He asked who I was and how I slept. I wiped my drenched face with the pea-green sleeve of my jacket. A breeze lifted the soft lines of the Japanese maple in the air. I wished I could pick up the stone and cradle it in my arms. I wished I could melt with it.

As I wept, my heart hardened. My own father wasn't here when we buried Jonah. He was overseas and had planned to leave that job—he could have been here. When Jonah was in the ICU, Ba left messages in a bothered voice, like he was owed good news. After the baby died, he wrote me uttering disappointment, and advised to contain my grief so not to worry others. Even though in childhood Ba hit me to stop me from crying, I had hoped my son mattered more than my father's peace and comfort.

I smoothed over the tombstone once more, and kissed my soiled fingertips. I placed them on the plaque. Now that Dr. Gordin recognized Jonah's life and my anguish, maybe he would know how to help me. He gave me something precious today: Compassion.

I got in the car and pulled napkins from the glove compartment to blow my nose. It was time to get Noah from school.

CHAPTER SIXTEEN

I shuffled carefully into the bathroom. A glass bottle dripped into a line attached to the inside of my elbow. My right arm stung as soon as I sat down. Fear rose with the ache at the IV site. Last week the infusion ended early because the catheter moved, causing an infiltration.

Oh, please stay in place.

It hurt more and more as I finished up and stood. Tiny webs of pink and green vessels rose under the stretched, pale skin of my lower arm. Unhooking the bottle from the stall and raising it above my heart so blood would not flow out, I rushed back to the IV Room.

"Diana! It's swelling." I got to my chair and rehung the bottle on a pole.

"Let's have a look." The nurse's gleaming blue eyes reminded me of a pair of marbles. Clear and cheerful. She rolled near me on a stool and peeled the tape off my arm.

"Maybe it's a false alarm. That's happened before." I peeked with her at the catheter.

Diana pressed around the inflated area and shook her head. "Sorry. It *is* infiltrated."

"It must have moved when I went to the bathroom." My brows furled.

Unlike fellow IVers, I had never gotten used to having a foreign object in my arm. I barely moved the arm to ensure the catheter's stay. "I only had half of it." I looked away as Diana pulled out the IV.

"Put a warm compress on the bump when you get home. It should go down in a day," she suggested.

The burning sensation subsided a little. A golf ball–size mount protruded, firm under the tender surface. The fluid went into the surrounding tissues instead of the vein.

"This is bad," I muttered.

"Your body is telling you something," Diana mused as she threw away the catheter in a red bio hazard box. Maybe you need a break from the IV."

"I can't. Without it I'm dead meat."

It had been eighteen months since I began the weekly infusion. I had almost passed out, warm-compressed, and often took multiple stabs. I drank twice as much water as the next patient to plump up the veins, which yielded trips to the bathroom during the procedure. It was stressful and barbaric yet gave me something to do for the MCS. It relieved fretting.

Diana said to take a break. Multiple chemical sensitivity did not take one. My body had spoken again. Sheer will did not always prevail.

~

"I can't live without the IVs." Two days later, I was in Dr. Gordin's office.

"Let's figure out how you can calm your body and mind. We assessed your stress hormone levels." He searched on the monitor on his desk for a report of my spit-in-the-tube test. "You wake up with a low alert level and crash at 3 p.m. The cortisol spikes at midnight."

"I'm a night owl. The later it gets, the clearer my head." Party time when all was dark and quiet.

"Then you don't sleep well."

"Right, and with the IV not working, I'm freaked out."

"We'll deal with this." He paused and glanced at me. "Remember we talked about relaxation?"

"Sorry, I never did the tai chi." I got found out.

"That's okay. Sometimes people aren't ready to do things. I just plant the seed," he said and grinned. "From the cortisol test results, it looks like you are on high alert at bedtime. You need to relax your brain and immune system. It may help with your sensitivity."

"I do everything I know of, except the relaxation." The *r* word was a mystery. I saw it as passive, doing nothing. Tai chi did not seem like relaxation. I had to *do* it.

"I got the mercury out of my mouth, I get the weekly IV, I eat clean ..." My broken record. Ah. I was repeating the same behavior in hope of a different outcome—Einstein's definition of insanity.

"Are you sleeping better?"

"No. This morning I dreamed that someone cut my hands open and blood was gushing out. It didn't hurt but I was startled and horrified."

"I want you to see Barbara." Dr. Gordin opened a file drawer next to his leg and pulled out a brochure.

"Who's Barbara? For what?"

"Learn re-lac-sation techniques."

The idea of spending more money with yet another health care provider constricted my stomach. "How many sessions do you think I need?"

"A few times. Until you learn to calm yourself. The goal is to rrr-rest your body," Dr. Gordin implored with open hands.

I glanced at the pink-bordered, tri-folded pamphlet. She was nearby, in Arlington ... something about transformation, learning disabilities, allergies, and career counseling. Did this person treat everything?

"I've already done a lot to detox," I said, dropping the brochure in my bag. What would Roger think?

"Everything you do helps. Eating a good diet, getting rid of mercury fillings, the IVs." Dr. Gordin offered up his palms again. "But the most important thing is to balance your sympathetic and parasympathetic nervous systems, and relax."

I wondered which "sympathetic" system did what. "So stop the IVs?"

"For now, stop for a month and then spread it out, every other week."

Oh my.

"Actually, I am only thirty-eight and shouldn't be tied to the IV for the rest of my life." I'd become so dependent on the infusion that I was hell bent on making it work. What if I were un-tethered, freed? I left the Marino Center full of possibilities.

~

The door was open in the home office. I found Roger in his usual seat, behind the laptop. I brought up Dr. Gordin's referral.

"We have to budget for this, Sue. Does she take insurance?" He turned from the screen.

"I don't think so. I doubt insurance covers hypnosis and neurolinguistic programming."

"What's that? Sounds weird."

"NLP?" I handed him the brochure.

He put it on top of a pile of papers. "We've burned through at least twenty thousand dollars for your chemical sensitivity." He stared. "Adding my dental revision, it was more like thirty."

"I'm feeling better, but you know I still get dizzy and I can't do the IV every week anymore." I fell back on the loveseat across from Roger.

"How many sessions will it take?"

"Dr. Gordin said 'a few.' I don't know—I've never done hypnosis before."

"Is it medically proven to help chemical sensitivity?"

"Maybe?" The large mahogany desk between us felt like a castle wall. "Dr. Gordin thinks I should calm my brain so I can sleep better. He says it can help the sensitivity."

"What does sleeping have to do with chemical sensitivity?" Roger shifted in his chair. "We don't have an infinite amount of money to keep trying new things. Is there an end point?"

His series of questions fired like a machine gun, popping my guilt. "Am I on the witness stand?" I raised my voice. "I'd love to know an end point myself!"

"I have the right to ask questions."

"Stop the lawyer speak." I met his sharklike eyes.

"As your husband, I deserve to know how we are spending money." Roger stood up and his nostrils flared.

"Of course you do." We had been partners, not master and servant like my parents. "I'm telling you why I need to spend. I don't want to be haunted by the next unseen chemical. I am out of ideas!" I jabbed at my chest, wishing it was a dagger.

"Why don't *you* worry about the finances?" Roger snapped. "Why do I always have to make up the difference?" I began to weep. "It's your money too, Sue. How you want to blow it is up to you."

"If I want to *blow it* I'd go to Hawaii." I had showed him my swollen arm from the bad IV. That was not enough. My shoulders hiccupped from containing the sobs. "I work hard to get better. There's no clear treatment for MCS. I wish it were a tumor. Then people ... you would accept what's involved."

"Poor you." His index finger pierced the air in front of me. "*You* come up with a plan. You can say, 'I don't know how this might work out, but maybe I'll try it three times and see if it helps.' Suggest *something*. Don't sit here crying like a baby."

I wiped my cheeks with the back of my hand. "I'm sick and upset and have to come up with a logical statement for spending? You have no empathy." Why did I bother to defend myself? Sorrow rose from my chest.

"Sue, you are not the same since Jonah died."

The mention of our deceased son clubbed me in the head. My despondency suddenly felt very familiar. It was like being in the NICU, watching the baby losing his heartbeat. Everything was broken. Out of control.

"Don't use Jonah's death against me." I knew that couples often split after losing a child, and maybe this was the crack in our dam. I glared at Roger. "And don't make me ask for money. I did that with my father when I was young."

He dropped back in his seat and went back to typing. "You are going to do whatever you want anyway. Just know that we don't have any savings for retirement or emergencies."

I couldn't see that far ahead. I felt ill *now*. Clearly he did not understand I was at another dead end. I got up and left.

I curled up in a chair in my study; I was the Girl Who Cried Wolf. Everything was a crisis. I wrote in my journal things like "Please let me have one clear-headed day. I'll do anything to get better but I am exhausted." I begged The One Above and Jonah's spirit to help. There were clues but no map.

It hurt to be shamed, called names, like I was subpar. Yet I could see how my desperation now could be construed as infantile. Growing up, I was punished for expressing my feelings. Having needs was shameful. I sucked it up. The buried problem would detonate when I could not withstand it anymore.

Roger and I had stood by each other during and since Jonah's passing. Before that we had balked at tradition and married outside of our Jewish and Taiwanese cultures. We were kindred spirits. We giggled playing squash. I loved his dry humor and integrity. If I was a baby, what did that make him? A parent? We play different roles in a committed relationship. We flowed between caring for and feeling cared for. I must have overstayed the "cared for" spot.

It was dinnertime. Whiffs of Ma's stir-fried shitake mushroom rice noodles permeated the air. I wished I was hungry.

Deep down I knew I was not a baby, even though for most of my life I believed what others said about me. Truth was a strange thing in a conflict. It was the sum of the participants' feelings and perceptions, a mirror of each other's disapproval and anxiety. We flung our contempt at each other like a hot potato. Granted I did not present Dr. Gordin's suggestion well tonight. But a baby would not keep looking for ways to get better.

I will make an appointment with that Barbara Johnson.

CHAPTER SEVENTEEN

"I feel anxious," I said.

"What do you see?" Barbara asked.

"Night. I hear voices."

"Let the anxiety build up in your chest. I'll count from ten to one. Let the feeling take you back to the earliest time that has everything to do with the anxiety," she suggested.

Do I do this? Lying in a black recliner, my body felt thick as I listened to the hypnotherapist's instructions. It was my third week learning relaxation techniques. In between our sessions, before bed I would listen to her tape counting slowly to ten; I would visualize going deep in the ground, feeling blank and heavy.

"Go back to your smallest self. Thirteen-year-old, ten-year-old, five- ..." her soft voice beckoned. I waded in the dark pool of the past.

"Adults are arguing ..." My heart pounded faster and louder.

"Do you see your hands? Are they big or small?"

"Small." Eyes closed, in my mind I saw my five-year-old fingers.

"What else?"

"We're huddled behind a wall or something big."

"Uh-huh."

"Taiwan-TV News fills a small screen on the top of a dresser." The image popped up in my head at random times and I could not decipher why. Now I knew. Something happened during the nightly news.

"Adults yelling ... loud." Agitation and worry surrounded me. "No, no." My breathing quickened. "No. Stop! Don't hit her. Stop." I whimpered through my inner child's throat. Tears streamed from the corners of my eyes. I could not make a peep when it happened. Seeing my caretaker argue and being struck shocked me to the core. My neck tightened. A wave of grief exploded in my head, chest, and spread to my extremities. "Baba hitting our mother. I want him to stop." Distress ate through my guarded wall. I needed to tell somebody.

"You poor thing. It's terrible." Barbara's gentleness came between my sobs.

"I stoop low with my younger sister and brother. We are scared. I keep them close." I whined.

"What else do you feel?"

"Helplessness. Desperate. I wish I can do something. No one can help us. No one." My nose dripped. I heard Barbara passing the tissue box near me. I reached for a tissue. "My mother is weeping. I despise my father."

I paused.

"Too much craziness," I continued. "The change in their voices scares me. Something bad is going to happen." Reclining under a heavy cotton blanket Barbara had placed over me, the movie of childhood filled my being.

"What would you like to say to your father?"

Dare I say anything? Last time I did I earned a crisp smack on the cheek. I was sixteen. A storm gathered in my heart. "You are an asshole for slapping and cursing at us." My eyelids, glued together by drying and new tears, were swollen from crying. "Wait. I am not allowed to speak to my father in English. Can I talk to him in Taiwanese?"

"Of course. You can say whatever you like, however you like." I heard Barbara take a swig of water.

In my seven-tone native tongue I unleashed on the father in my recollection: "YOU go to hell. Leave us alone. YOU are the motherfucker, not us. You stop cursing. You hurt everybody." I pictured shoving him away, for me, my siblings, and my mother. I raged and ranted until I ran out of things to say. Part of me wondered if this was the brain-calming Dr. Gordin ordered. "Okay," I told Barbara. "I scolded and pushed him back."

"Good," Barbara said.

How would this help me? "I am done for now," I said. The buttery chair under me and I had fused into one.

"Ready to come back?"

"Yes."

"You are coming down, lower and lower. You see the clouds, the mountains. You'll wake up feeling refreshed, remembering everything. I'm going to count back from five." She sucked in her breath. "Five ... hands and legs are getting bigger. Four ... bigger and bigger. Three ... you'll open your eyes when I count to one. Two ... your eyelids are moving. One ... welcome back."

As if I landed the space shuttle. Barbara had brought me home from galaxies beyond. I blinked and a haze of green faded from view. I put on my glasses. Barbara's cornflower blue eyes shined. I pushed the recliner to the sitting position.

"What was that? I thought I came to learn relaxation. It was all over the place. I had no idea that childhood was going to come up." I had to remember my reason for seeing Barbara.

"In hypnosis, you *are* relaxing. Your immune system gets a break and it'll thank you. Every day, listen to the tape I made you. Your body will calm down."

"Will it help the chemical sensitivity, the dizziness, the brain fog?"

"I think so."

"Are you sure?" I asked. It was too good to be true. No needles.

"Soothing your mind helps the body. Sure."

I wanted to believe her. "What about these childhood issues I just dumped? It's okay?"

"Of course."

Irony washed over me. Roger's sarcasm rang in my head: *She is paid to say what you want to hear.* So what? This could be my chance. "If the stuff that bothers me—the junk, comes out, that's okay?"

"If you want it to come out, yes."

"Great. Clean it all out." I waved away an imaginary fly in front of me. "I want everything out. I am tired of nightmares and waking up exhausted."

"We can do that," Barbara chirped.

I had never met a therapist like this. She let me run over twenty minutes and was grinning. Usually the counselor stopped me in the middle of a sentence with a stone face and announced, "Time's up, see you next week."

After talking about my life in the present, such as my work and Noah, I got up. In the softly lit office, Barbara gave me a hug.

Like a bee hovering over a flower after collecting nectar, I lingered outside her office building under its faint porch light. Was she for real? Her generosity and kindness perplexed me. I was not used to people being *this* nice to me.

I must have trusted her. I let her see my Taiwanese child self and exposed the percolating wreck inside, unbeknownst even to me. I had accumulated layers of defense atop the semblance of a "normal" life: degrees, a job, a family, a nice car.

The cool autumn night air woke my senses. A few dry leaves next to my feet shuffled away as I walked. I took a deep breath.

Holy cow. My chest felt lighter than it ever had before.

CHAPTER EIGHTEEN

"I just walked into a corner," I said, dragging myself across the master bedroom to Roger's office. The two rooms shared a wall.

"Sorry to hear that, sweetie. Going to bed?" Roger looked up, laptop screen reflected on both lenses of his glasses. Piles of paper and manila folders surrounded the computer, making a nest.

"Yeah. I need it." I rubbed my forehead. At eleven o'clock, MCS fatigue kicked in.

"I need to finish this contract for a client. It will probably take an hour."

That meant two hours. I shut the door to the office and slithered between the flannel sheets in our bedroom. Our bed faced the halogen-induced daylight that seeped under the door. I yanked the comforter up to my chin. Barbara's voice streamed through the ear bud from my little tape player. I drifted off.

Ro-ro-ro ...

Ro-ro-ro ... Ka-LUMP!

Like ball bearings sliding on a rusty track ...

I stirred.

The drawer in Roger's desk.

I turned and grabbed the alarm clock on the night table next to me. Twelve forty. Midnight was my threshold. Dr. Gordin said I needed sleep. I wanted to sleep. Near the foot of our bed, the spring on the doorknob turned and clicked. I made out Roger's shadow.

CREAK. Creak. The wood floor responded to his weight.

Roger knew I was a light sleeper, and I had asked him to be quiet. Not sure if he remembered. My communication felt like the door, hollow and doing a poor job. Flying monkeys released in my head: Roger must not respect me.

My father used to call me a sleeping pig when he barged in on non-school days, ripping open curtains and announcing "Sun's shining on your behind." My siblings followed with the song "Wake up, Little Susie."

"Can you be quiet?" I yelled. It was like asking the hare to go at a turtle's pace. My husband moved with swift purpose.

"Sorry," he whispered loudly.

Jolted from stupor, I felt if he didn't do what I asked, then he must not care. I turned away when he got in bed.

We had a different understanding of what was late and what was loud. As a boy, Roger had his own room and schedule. He stayed up as he pleased. I roomed with my sister. I was quiet. I trained with the master, Ma, who could disappear in a roomful of wakeful people. Roger tried to be quiet. He just was not. He logged long hours and coped with me. The MCS had drained our funds and energy. It was not my place to say when he could work.

I frowned into the cold, black air. It hung dense like Jell-O. Roger's rhythmic breathing revealed he had left the human realm. I gazed at the back of his head. Lucky him. Another half hour went by. I finally dozed and dreamed:

My hands clutched a glass table and pulled it toward me. At the other end was my father, lugging it toward him. Behind him was a stucco arch extended to a wrought iron balcony. Red geraniums filled terra-cotta urns set on the ground. It was Italy, where my parents, Roger, and I went a few months after Jonah died.

Ba and I were in a tug-of-war. I let go of the table because I didn't want to pull anymore. My father slid back and fell off the balcony. My mother looked over the railing and said in Taiwanese, "His head is bleeding." My father was dead.

I gasped in horror and woke up. Stomach tight, I wanted to cry out but nothing came. Our trip to Italy was meant for a reprieve after losing a child. Instead we became referees between my parents. They fought despite promises of not arguing on the trip. I shook off the dream and got out of bed.

Sunlight oozed through the crevices around the room-darkening blinds. The space next to me was empty. Roger had returned to his office. The door was closed again.

~

"How can I sleep better? I am a jumpy sleeper. I dream all the time." In the black recliner, I gestured at Barbara. The afternoon glowed in a window behind her, contrasting a poster on the wall of a black mountain in a red sky.

My mother had kept us from going to kindergarten so we could sleep more. Why did she think we didn't get enough? Good rest was an elusive breath I could not catch. I had tried sleeping pills after losing Jonah. One rough night I took an Ambien with Advil for a headache and ended up in the Emergency Room for hallucinations. Drugs were not an option for me now anyway because of the MCS.

"This morning I dreamed I killed my father." I described the dream. "I don't know why he appeared. He belongs to the past."

"That sounds awful. Beliefs can stay the same over time. What belief do you think your dream is expressing?" Barbara brushed through her spiked auburn hair.

"If I stop engaging, somebody dies? I'm responsible for my father's life?" Repulsion rose from my gut. I was eternally on the hook. I already had my mother on my list. Ba *too*?

"Do you believe that?" Barbara asked.

"No, no-no. So why am I dreaming it?" I clutched the arms of the chair.

"You have an interesting relationship with your subconscious. Let's find out." She inched her chair toward me. "Ready for some hypnosis?"

Barbara draped the cotton blanket on me, covering my body from neck to toe. In the reclining position, I exhaled. Instructions of relaxation poured out of her mouth. Minutes later, I felt anchored to the chair.

"You said you felt bad in your stomach when you woke up with this nightmare. Can you feel it now?"

"Yes," I mumbled.

"Let it get strong and stronger."

My gut twisted. I started to pant as my heartbeat raced. The noose on my throat tightened. *Bring it.* I had nothing to lose.

"Now I'll count to five. Let your arms get smaller and smaller."

In the mind's eye, I saw that.

"One, hands getting smaller too ... Two, fingers too ... Five, are your arms really small?"

"Yes." I was a young child again. A sense of doom descended upon me.

"Are you inside or outside?"

"Inside."

"How old are you?"

"Four or five."

"Are you still anxious?"

"Very. It's dark, and I don't like it. There are other kids with me." My breath quickened.

Not this again. I did this before.

"What is happening?"

I whined from my leaden head, "I am scared. I must watch out for my sister and brother. I want my parents to stop." Tears streamed down my face.

"What do you see?"

I did not want to *see*. I knew. "Ma and Ba arguing ..."

Barbara handed me a tissue. "That's terrible. Can you separate your parents and have each one of them sitting on the opposite side of the room?"

"No. I just want them to stop."

"How about you look at your mother?"

My mother's young face flashed into my head. Sadness and bewilderment filled her large almond-shaped eyes.

"She wants me to say who's right in the argument. She wants me to know that she suffered for her kids." My body convulsed with grief.

"What do you want to say to your mother?"

"Ma, you have to stand up for yourself. Do something!" I pleaded with her face in my head. The reply was a blank look. There was no soul behind her round, reddened features. Her eyes looked like mine.

"Would you like to role-play your mother?"

"Yuck, no. She is such a sad person." I stuck out my tongue. Maggots came to mind.

"Sometimes we learn from our parents. What they do or believe is also in us. Talking as them helps us to understand them. Would you like to try?"

"Well, okay." I dabbed my wet face with a tissue.

Barbara tapped on my shoulder. "Now you are Mom. What would you like to say to the young Sue?"

In the darkness of hypnosis, a black-and-white image of me from eons ago emerged. Round faced, pouty lips with pudgy legs. I began in my native tongue. "Shogi (Sue-Yi)-ah, very sorry. I try make okay for you kids. I stay with your father for you three. No other way. Remember, rely on yourself." It rolled out of my mouth. I got quiet in my surprise.

"Now I'll tap you again," Barbara said. I heard her drink from her water bottle. "You are Sue now. What would you say to your mother?"

"Thank you for trying, Ma. I know you couldn't help what happened but you should do something for yourself." I understood my mother's intentions. Strange.

"Would you forgive your mother?"

"No. I am mad now. I hate her helplessness."

"When you hold a grudge, it takes a lot of energy."

"I can't let it go at this moment." I sneered.

"Okay. Ready to come back?" Barbara told me to see my hands getting bigger and to remember everything. She counted backwards and I opened my eyes.

"That was a lot of sobbing." I sighed and tossed balls of soaked tissues in the trash.

"How do you feel?" Barbara passed me the tissue box.

"Wiped out. But my chest feels lighter again. Hey ... this works!" I wiped my puffy eyes. "So it wasn't a fluke last time. I never thought mental anguish is connected to the body this way." In my head, a beam illuminated a green mountainscape. Barbara had unveiled something.

"Why did I go back to this fighting scene again? We did this last time."

"Maybe you want to work it out. Like recurring dreams. Sometimes people keep playing the same theme in the dreams until they resolve or understand the message."

"Why can't I forgive my mother? Will I stop having bad dreams? Why would I have nightmares about causing my father's demise—he is the villain here." Maybe I was stuck in my child self's narcissistic worldview. I still believed I was responsible for my parents' lives. They said I was. They stayed married because of me and my siblings.

"We'll find out. It sounds cliché, but it is like peeling the onion. When you are ready, the next layer will reveal itself. For now, practice the relaxation every day," Barbara said.

"I've got a big can of worms."

"You released something big tonight. Make sure you get extra rest."

"Barbara, releasing this garbage feels good. But what does it have to do with the chemical sensitivity?"

"Like I mentioned before, hypnosis or deep relaxation gives your immune system a chance to rest." She paused and sucked in her breath, a trait I really liked for no reason. "You don't have to hold everything in your body."

I dipped my chin in thought.

Barbara stood up and gave me a hug. "You're doing well."

I raised my brows at the clock behind her. "It's way past our time. Sorry."

"That's okay. You were in the middle of something and needed to finish."

I floated out of her office in gratitude. I thought I would discuss IVs and learn more relaxation techniques. Instead, I discovered that I carried a truckload of hurt, along with my mother, for years. It had caused us both to hunch over. My father had threaten to tie a washboard on my back.

I hold it in my body. The physical and mental, the mind and body, how did the two relate?

On the drive home, a light rain misted the street. Everything glistened under street lamps. Drops clustered on my windshield, making round, magnified outlines around cars and traffic lights.

My eyes filled with tears as my tires rolled on the noisy, wet pavement. I was guilty of birth, the reason my mother struggled. Her claim also enraged me. How could I be accountable for something I had no say in? Our Taiwanese culture endorsed the breadwinner. What was she supposed to do?

I pulled the car into our driveway and sat in the frigid autumn evening. I recalled my parents "conferenced" late nights about Ba's infidelity and job changes. Once I woke to Ma raising a boom box over her head blaring Tchaikovsky. "I'm going to smash it if you don't stop playing with women!" she yelled. I huddled with my sister and brother in the doorway. My ears had scanned for disagreements in the next room. As a child, I slept on egg shells. After Jonah died and Noah came, I slept on egg shells. Now struggling with chemicals, smells, food, and noises, *I still sleep on egg shells.* "Damn!" I pounded the steering wheel. Barbara said, beliefs had no time limit. Home was never a place to relax—it was where conflicts and fear danced. I, a sack of traumas, continued to carry angst and spread it for posterity.

I would never have thought about this if my health was intact.

Closing the car door, I looked up at the house. Lights radiated from our large rectangular living room windows. It called to me like a moth to fire. I unlocked the door to Noah's running feet thumping across the hardwood floor.

CHAPTER NINETEEN

I could not wait to get there—the place where I pushed Noah's stroller during soft winter mornings, where I met with friends and we shared meals with our babies.

"This is going to be fun." I broke out in a smile as Burlington Mall's tan exterior emerged beyond the exit ramp.

Roger parked the car and exited the driver's side. "There's nowhere I'd rather be on a Saturday afternoon," he joked.

"I know, I know. You get tired when we go to the mall, but I appreciate you coming. I wonder how I'll feel after getting into the stores." Eighteen months ago, standing at the doors of Sears and CVS sent me into a nauseating tizzy.

Ma stepped up to us. "Shogi, we go Verizon first."

My mother was the reason we came. She needed a new phone and an ear bud. We entered the shopping complex via the dress section at Lord & Taylor. Willowy mannequins wore vibrant spring fashions and I marveled at their colors and cheer. Odors of new dresses greeted me. The garment industry used sizing, chemicals that kept clothes fresh and unwrinkled. I scanned for an escape route. The path dividing the cosmetics counters led to the mall concourse.

"I'll meet you at Verizon's." Holding my breath, I zipped by Roger and Ma.

As I reached the glass-roofed expanse, I exhaled. Two teenagers in skinny jeans sauntered by in a cloud of perfume. I cringed at the odor and touched my right index finger with my thumb, a gesture I'd been practicing with Barbara to signal my body to relax. *It's okay. It's only a slight smell.* A little foggy, I parked myself on a bench across from the Verizon counter and waited.

Ma got in line. Roger sat next to me and held my hand.

"Hmm." I closed my eyes and took in the sounds of children, footsteps, and a roaring mechanical alligator that popped up from a man-made swamp every five minutes at the Rainbow Café. I had missed coming here. I liked the energy of lively displays and shoppers. I craved the freedom to go anywhere.

Ma walked toward us. "Shogi-ah, Verizon thief. Steal money. Sign say earphone on sale. The cashier say no. I try tell her. She say no."

I got back in line with Ma. After at least three roars from the giant plastic reptile, we approached the counter and Jennifer, the customer service rep.

"The sign at the shelf said fifteen percent off on the ear buds. Why didn't my mother get the discount?" I asked.

"You have to buy two to get the discount," Jennifer replied.

"The sign did not say you have to buy two. Isn't that Verizon's mistake? Could you give her the discount?" We were negotiating a dollar and fifty cents.

"Your mom already got her sign-up discount."

"Are you saying because she got one discount she isn't entitled to another?" My eyebrows rose above my glasses.

She looked behind us, where the line was growing. "No. But she has to buy two of those to get the discount."

Her repetition of the policy, without consideration, incensed me.

Ma pulled at my arm. "Ah-yah, forget it. Only dollar fifty."

I turned and saw Roger's scowl from the bench. I left the courtesy counter with Ma in tow. "I have been at the mall. I feel seventy percent, a little woozy. Verizon sucks. Let's go," I proclaimed.

"Sue, will you be quiet?" My husband stood up.

"I am not happy about what they did." I crossed my arms. "I'm speaking up. Is that a problem for you?"

"There is a time and a place," he stared.

We got back in the car. Roger drove by rows of sedans and SUVs, then the tree-lined highway. Every branch whipped by my side like a slap in the face. I said to him, "You don't need to educate me. I'm an adult."

"I'm just giving you feedback."

I rolled my eyes at the windshield. "Verizon wasn't fair or truthful to my mother."

"You can speak up *nicely.*"

"I started that way. The rep acted like we were wasting her time."

"These people aren't the highest paid, best-trained people. What do you expect?"

"I expect honesty, and I am aware that Jennifer was seeing two Asian women haggling with her over a dollar and fifty cents."

"I don't know if it's a race thing."

"We appear a certain way to her and she appears a certain way to us. Goes both ways." Living in America taught me this.

"I don't understand this anger," Roger said.

"Shogi-ah, since therapy you turn nasty," Ma chimed in from the back.

~

The next day my hands flew in the air as I shared the incident with Barbara.

"Have you ever heard of the crabs in a pot?" she said.

"No." I leaned back in the black recliner.

"When you are healing and changing, sometimes people around you don't understand it or want you to change.

Sometimes they say or do things to bring you back to the old place. Like the crabs. One climbs up toward the top of the pot to leave, the others pull it back down."

"Like people are used to having me going along?" I was raised to comply. Lately I found it was not who I *am*.

Barbara nodded and sipped her latte. Its aroma made the room cozy. "You are taking ownership of your feelings and you will figure out how to express them. It's like learning to ride a bicycle. You'll get better at it. Someday you can even say things to people you are mad at with ease."

"That would be fabulous."

May I speak without fear.

"What about this anger Roger mentioned? What makes you angry?" Barbara flung a golden wrap around her shoulders and pulled it over her chest.

"Huh?" I muttered. It took me a year to admit I was angry when I worked with another therapist post-Jonah. "I was defending my mother. Too many unfair events and people ... they make me angry."

"Do you think the anger gets in the way of relaxation?"

"Of course."

"Let's do some hypnosis." Barbara moved her chair toward me. "Focusing on relaxing."

"It's hard to relax. I need to take care of everyone else first so I don't have to worry." I pulled at my wedding ring. "I got mad about the Verizon rep. I had to fix that, and there's always more to fix."

"Seems like lots to do before you can relax."

"I feel guilty when I let go, like I should do something useful instead. My mother used to disapprove of my writing letters to friends or reading novels. The fun stuff. She wanted me to read textbooks and get good grades. If I didn't do that, I got disapproval and nagging." My chest started to tense.

"Do you have this belief—that relaxation or having fun is bad?"

"I guess."

"In hypnosis we deal with deep-seated beliefs, beliefs that were instilled in you subconsciously or when you were young. When we change those beliefs, the behaviors will change. Symptoms will go away."

I liked symptom free. If clearing my closet of traumas led to wellness and freedom, I was game.

"Let's do this: How about using one of your hands to represent 'hard to relax' and the other 'relaxed'?"

"Interesting." I looked at the empty hands on my lap.

"What would you like the intention to be for today?"

"I want to clear my guilt about relaxing, and clear that anger." I pushed the back of the recliner to its lowest position. Barbara chanted her instructions and I closed my eyes.

"Now imagine you are going up in the sky, higher and higher, past the clouds and mountains," she began.

"No ... I can't. I often dream about falling in a plane."

"How about going down the stairs, lower and lower, relaxing every step of the way?"

"Sorry, I have nightmares of being trapped underground too." My head got tight, losing the tranquil feeling.

"What might work for you?"

"Whatever I want?" I felt sheepish about resisting. "I'd love to be in a warm, sunny field with wildflowers. A friendly place."

"Sounds good. Picture yourself there." Barbara's chair creaked. "Are you there?"

"Yes. It's nice. I am in a golden bubble filled with bright rays. Warm sunshine on my skin."

"Excellent. Let's get back to your hands," she continued. "One is relaxed, and one is not."

"The one that is uptight is very upset." I spoke like a wooden puppet.

"Why is it upset?"

"Because it was hit by a mean teacher in second grade. I was twenty points away from getting the one hundred so I was hit twice. Those who got seventy got hit three times, and so on." I was surprised this came up. "Before that class started, I was in the playground with classmates rubbing orange peels on our palms, hoping it would relieve the sting of the bamboo whip we knew was coming."

"It is wrong to hit a child. I'm sorry you went through that."

"Everyone was in the same boat. Our parents said the teacher was always right. If we were hit, we must have been bad." Taiwanese children were considered raw jade, to be polished and carved by teachers.

"So you got hit in school and no one from home was going to protect you."

"That's right. I had no one." Tears rushed to my eyes. "I had a dream where my hands got sliced open by a big knife. Blood gushed out and I just watched it, shocked."

"You poor thing. That's just awful." Barbara paused. "Would you like to talk to your teacher—what's her name?"

"Chen Tzun-Zhi. Model teacher from hell ... I think every 'good' teacher in Taiwan then believed in hurting students in the name of excellence."

"Stay with the unhappy student in you, Sue. Try not to think." Later I learned that thinking during hypnosis allowed the conscious mind to take over and I would pop out of the trance.

"Before I tell my teacher off, I have more stories about school."

"Go ahead."

"One day I didn't finish my lunch on time and still had a pear my mother packed. I knew my mother would be upset if I didn't finish the food. After class started, I bent over and bit the fruit. Teacher Chen had me stand up and scolded me in the class of fifty kids. She ordered me to open my mouth and put a chalk in between my teeth ... told me to stand that way until the bell rang." I cried as humiliation and terror filled Barbara's office.

"That's horrific, Sue. She had no right to do that. That's abusive."

"I wanted to finish my lunch. I forgot the rules." Eyes still closed, I accepted several tissues from Barbara and blew my nose. "One time she dragged me by the ear in front of the class because I didn't stop playing with something. I didn't know where my body would end up." I wailed.

How could I weep about what happened thirty years ago? It felt real at the moment.

"You have no one to turn to. What do you do?" Barbara asked.

"I make sure I know the rules and *make no mistakes*. Be on guard, perfect, and invisible."

"That's a lot for an eight-year-old. Could the adult you talk to and comfort the young Sue in elementary school?"

"I don't want to go near her. She's pathetic." My younger version, untouched and un-thought of, was a pariah.

"What does she look like? Can you describe her?"

"She's sad. Nobody cares about her. As long as she is a good student and daughter, she is left alone. And left alone is peachy. Beats scorn and nitpicking."

"Can you say something positive about the little Sue?"

My teachers said I talked too much. My mother said I did not worry enough, that I was conceited like my father. I slouched. Little Sue grossed me out.

Several minutes went by.

Barbara cleared her throat. "Sue?"

Oh. Something good about the young me. "Maybe ... she is cute. She has big, wide-set eyes and shiny, straight hair. She makes faces. She likes to have fun."

"Yeah. I bet she does," Barbara cajoled. "Can the adult you speak to her now?"

"Umm. Little Sue-Yi ... this is very weird. Umm, I'm very sorry that you had to live with a cruel teacher and unaware parents. I'm sorry you were all alone. You did a good job in school and Teacher Chen is just rotten. It isn't your fault." I sniffled. "I'll take care of you now."

"Great," Barbara interjected. "Tell her that you'll never let her go. That she's going to be okay. She's going to grow up and go to Wellesley and Harvard, have a family."

I never looked at my life that way. I did all right.

Barbara continued, "When you take care of your younger self, she will give you back *everything*. That's not the case when you take care of other people. Would you like to give little Sue a hug?"

In my mind, I embraced the school girl in her white shirt and navy blue skirt. I stroked her soft black hair. "She feels relieved," I said.

"Ex-cellent!" Barbara said. "Would you like to speak to your teacher now?"

"Gladly." I adjusted my neck in the recliner and recalled the freckles on my teacher's flat nose. "You terrorize a bunch of second-graders. You are a bully!" Ranting in English to my Taiwanese teacher was strange too. No matter. "You're not perfect either but you demand it from a group of defenseless kids. You and your whipping stick can go back to hell!"

"Good for you, Sue. No one should treat children the way your teacher did. Ever. Anything else you'd like to say to this teacher?"

"No. I am done with her. Now I want to talk about my father."

"What about him?"

"Remember I said I had straight, shiny hair? It's like his hair. I got his hair. One time he blow-dried it and told me it was soft like a canary's feathers." In my mind I saw us in a mirror in our Taipei apartment. He held the hairdryer over my head.

"That's sweet."

"It was one of the few times he was nice to me. He mostly acted like he was stuck with us. We cost him money and food. When he got mad, we got belted. There was no unconditional love. Everything was conditional. I wanted him to like me. I waited for him to come home when he traveled for work, which was often." I scrunched the tissue in my fist. Another flood of tears rained down my face. "I feel guilty hating him ... or liking him."

Admitting having feelings for the Devil of the family was a betrayal to the rest of its members. It was impossible to love my father like the way it was to keep Jonah.

"Ba was vicious. There is this family picture. We were at a zoo and I was two. My mother held my infant sister in her arms. She and my father smiled for the picture. I was teary-eyed with a handkerchief dangling off my hand." I swallowed. "I wanted to see the elephants. My father said giraffes were on the way and we would go there first. I kept asking for the elephants. He slapped me so I'd stop insisting. Then he snapped the picture."

"That's terrible. Children should not be hit, no matter what," Barbara implored. "I am sorry, Sue. Would you like to say something to him?"

"Ba, I am scared to death most of the time and have to guess what you like." I turned toward Barbara's direction. "I want to hit him back."

"Good. Here's a big pillow. You can punch it to get out your feelings." She put it on my lap. My fingers brushed over its ribbed texture.

"You jerk!" Eyes shut, I yelled aloud and pummeled it several times. "I don't owe you! I don't deserve the hitting and heartlessness."

Silence came after the fireworks.

"Anything else, Sue?"

"No. I'm pooped."

Barbara brought me out of my trance after telling me to remember everything. We chatted a bit to ensure I was in the present. She commended me on the work I had done.

"I can't believe what started out with my hands about relaxation resulted in all this other stuff. Thank you."

"It was good to get a sense of your family, to put you in context." Barbara got up. "We've uncovered a lot about the guilt and anger today."

"We didn't work directly on relaxation."

"Everything is related and will have a way of working itself out."

The vagueness concerned me. I suppressed more questions and grinned. I had been there for over two hours.

"Listen to your tape twice a day and go to the sunny garden in your mind. Make friends with the little girl Sue."

It was a tall order. Instinctively I still wanted to run from the girl within, even after our hug in the trance today. But the goody-goody in me decided to beat the old pattern, in gratitude to Barbara. I drove home in the dusk. Headlights on the road enlarged and slid out of my periphery. I considered my homework of liking my inner child, who was buried under layers of traumas and anger.

She existed.

At bedtime Roger and I held hands under the comforter. I told him about the long session and that after releasing some ancient horror, I saw the little girl in me, the exuberant one.

Roger wrapped his arm over me. "She comes out once in a while," he said.

"That was the girl you fell in love with." I caressed his fuzzy arm. "I think Barbara is doing a great job."

"Sounds like it."

"I'm finding lots of stuff from childhood. I didn't think it mattered."

Roger burrowed his head next to mine.

"It's like skimming the surface of an oil spill. There's so much crap hiding beneath." I tugged at the hair on his arm. "You think I'll be able to empty out everything and start over? I would be free, from MCS and nightmares."

One snore, then another.

"Rog?" Whenever I gabbed in bed, he relaxed. Savoring the licorice warmth from his body, I shut off the lamp.

It was the first night I slept without nightmares.

CHAPTER TWENTY

Ascending the stairwell I used to climb daily, I smiled in anticipation. I could ace this interview. But, if I got the job, could I handle it?

I settled into the mint-green sofa next to a lead window and addressed my ex-boss, the director of the Center for Work and Service.

"I'm so sorry to hear that Carol passed away—what a shock," I said.

"It was. I'm sad about it." Joanne's ice blue eyes focused on me. She flipped back her shoulder-length hair, revealing an amethyst earring framed in gold.

"That must have been hard for the staff too." I clasped my hands to feel myself. *I can't believe I'm doing this.*

"You wrote that you are interested in coming back to work with us."

"Yes, I'd like to explore that with you." After Noah's brief hospitalization at one month old, I quit the associate director post to be home full-time. Carol took over but recently had a stroke in her sleep.

I continued, "In the last four years I've been running data collection for research projects. The job has changed due to funding. I also miss counseling students and being on campus."

"How is your health? I heard you were sick," Joanne said.

I knew this would come up. I had bowed out of serving on a committee for the CWS when the chemical sensitivity rendered me unable to read freshly copied applications.

"I'm better. I get vitamin C IVs and work with a hypnotherapist weekly. It's night and day. My head's clear now." Or clear enough. I rattled off treatments and interventions I had done over the past two years as Joanne nodded. I needed to convince myself I was up to the task.

"The thing is, Joanne, I want to do more than word processing and making phone calls. I miss doing workshops and helping people with career and life decisions."

"Are you sure? We have a staff of sixteen and LOTS of events." Joanne stretched back the corners of her mouth and her shoulders at the same time. A familiar gesture. "I want someone who leads and creates innovative programming. I want a right-hand person."

Me. Me! As the eldest in my family, I negotiated between siblings and parents. I was *both* hands. "I'd enjoy creating new programs with you again," I said. I knew Joanne demanded effort and loyalty. The more her people did, the better she looked. "I'd love to work with you and this staff."

My colleagues here were friends. They went through life and death with me. Post-Jonah, Joanne and the staff took extra care to put away items from my office that would remind me of the pregnancy. She sent me home after seeing my puffy eyes and pale face at a meeting in this very conference room. And when Noah arrived, he was received like family.

"I have more life experiences to offer as a career counselor." I could not stop selling.

Suddenly I realized that an exciting world existed beyond my bucolic office at Cheever House. At CWS I could coordinate a team of counselors, see students, and teach workshops instead of collecting surveys and being a gopher to my study directors. When my brain was fuzzy, I could only coast and hope my assignments were simple. Now they gnawed at me.

My mind had woken up from the MCS haze.

"I'd love this job," I said.

Joanne smiled. "Good, I'm glad." Her fair coloring and tall frame exuded charisma. She cast a spell I had forgotten. I wanted to say yes to everything she asked for.

Wait. The current Sue was not the old Sue. The MCS was not completely gone. I needed to watch it—I could still get overtired.

"What exactly do you expect from the associate director?" I asked.

"The position has grown since you held it. I want the workshops standardized, policies and protocols for the counseling staff written, someone in charge of the overall outreach to students, the day-to-day counseling and drop-ins ... and someone who helps me with strategic planning, staff development, and faculty outreach. We can do something great."

I grinned, happy that she knew my potential. But the MCS and my tendency to bite off more than I could chew dried my throat. The career services at Wellesley College had a large staff for its student body. Its output was much bigger too.

"Uh ... Is the position still half-time?"

"Yes," she replied. "Seventeen and a half hours a week. We've posted it in several places and many people asked for full-time, but that's not in the budget." Her eyes flashed back at me.

"I would like part-time." With health concerns and a young child, I preferred this schedule. I recalled Joanne's penchant for the latest and greatest. I used to stay late and on weekends, pre-children, pre-MCS. Would I be able to do it now?

"You met the staff last week. I heard good things from the group interview." She sat back in her chair and beamed.

The staff had hugged me and giggled when I came up to the office. One of the newer assistants, who I did not know, likened it to a "Second Coming." They were quirky, well-meaning women. A group of souls who understood each other and cared about the students.

"The position sounds really interesting. I'll be good at it," I assured her.

Joanne's face brightened. "Great. I'll talk to H.R. When can you start?"

We discussed logistics and compensation. I would go into the office three days a week, and probably telecommute at times, which was a good schedule. We ended the meeting with a cheery embrace. Her stature and warmth wrapped around me, as if I were coming home.

I half sprinted down the hall and stairs. My heart fluttered. If I did not have MCS, I would be completely elated. Would the stress of this new job cause a major flare-up? Would I fall apart again? With Joanne, my work related to the entire staff. If I turned green and could not handle the smell of printouts, it would be a bigger disaster than my current situation, where I had a well-defined role that anyone could do in a pinch. But I wanted to lead, have my own office, and use my head. Maybe Barbara could help me figure it out.

Once at home, I fired off three e-mails to Barbara. The first asked whether I was well enough to take on a management job. We had been working together for nineteen months, and an opportunity was upon me. The second missive said I was not sure if I could handle more responsibility but really wanted it. The last listed the pros and cons of the new position.

"What's happening, busy bee?" Barbara's reply began. "What does your intuition say?"

Relieved about her willingness to engage in cyberspace, I contemplated the question. The intuition was a concept I learned from Barbara. It was a gut feeling, the first thing one felt without too much thinking. In one session, she asked me if I had ever done something just going with it and ended up okay. Yes, I recalled in my twenties, being stranded in Manhattan after clubbing and stayed at some male premed student's uncle's flat in Jersey. It was not my finest moment, probably my worst. I was lucky I was not raped and left in a dumpster.

"For someone like you to do that ... you knew you would be safe for some reason," Barbara said.

Indeed. On my hunch I had chosen a decent life partner despite having terrible role models. I had found a career I enjoyed. After applying to mostly engineering programs, I went to a liberal arts college and loved it.

I could hear Barbara's voice in my head: "What if you use your instinct by choice? Check in with your feelings."

She taught me to seek answers from myself many times in hypnosis.

Finding the intuition was like bottling an omniscient spirit. I got up from the desk and sank into my leather chair.

I'll have a conversation with Barbara now—in my mind. It's faster.

"You were terrorized as a child, as we have acknowledged in our sessions. Do you think it's okay to have feelings?" Barbara would say.

"Of course."

"What's your feeling about taking this job at the career center?" She would follow up.

"That I want it?"

"Can you do the work?"

"I think I can." *I have Barbara. I slept better. I learned a few tools to deal with stress.*

"Don't think. Feel."

"Okay. I feel ..." I paused. "I feel I can!"

"Now, trust this feeling. It'll keep you safe. You can change your mind and navigate as you go. How does that feel?"

"Feels solid."

"Good. The solid feeling is what you go by. What does that feel like?"

"A firm, connected feeling in my stomach and chest, very different from the superficial, in-the-moment yearning to please Joanne."

"Ex-cellent!" I could hear Barbara holler her favorite word.

"Do I need to worry about the chemical sensitivity?"

"What does your intuition say?"

"Don't worry, you're covered! But ... what does the intuition have to do with MCS? How would it help me in the job?"

"Perhaps you are always on guard, defending yourself, and constantly on the lookout for offenders. This algorithm helped you survive when you were a young child. You had to be perfect. Over time it made you sick. You don't need to operate this way anymore." Barbara would pause and draw in a breath. "What if you connect to your intuition, relax, and stop looking out for chemicals or people hurting you? Trust. Do the work you love. Wouldn't that be nice?"

Super nice. I chuckled at the abundant answers coming from nowhere. A brilliant light flipped on in my mind and a voice sang, "Laaaah." Intuition felt like instant joy in connectedness and self-knowledge.

I returned to the laptop and pounded away on the keyboard, replying to Barbara's e-mail with what I just figured out: I was ready and would go with my instinct to become the associate director at CWS.

CHAPTER TWENTY-ONE

December descended and it was near Jonah's birthday. His was a reminder of what could have been. Holiday lights wrapped around trees and windows, cheer broadcasted from television and radio. A time for family reunions. I should have enjoyed more his ten-month stay in the womb, his only home on earth, because after he left it he was in an ambulance flying in the night, then in a clear bassinette in newborn intensive care, and lastly in a white box.

Our story was sad but at least we had one. Today I asked Barbara for help in finding relief from the sorrow, especially between Thanksgiving and New Year's Day. This year was extra poignant because our quest for justice for Jonah in court had come to an abrupt end, adding a load on my mind and body. I felt robbed.

I could have been a nicer mommy to Jonah. I regretted disliking my huge belly when I hunched over it on the bed to work on my laptop. I was keen to finish projects before going into labor. I got irritated that he kicked inside while I typed outside. I thought we had a lifetime together. When my aunt saw Jonah in the NICU and said he resembled me, I quickly denied it. I did not wish Jonah to favor the Taiwanese side. I wanted half and half. I hoped for him to be cuter, unlike my father, the male version of me.

After my long hours of labor, the obstetrician offered me Pitocin to stimulate the contractions. Then an epidural, higher dose of it, more Pitocin, and forceps. She put the wrong length of forceps around Jonah's head, clamped hard, and pulled.

Jonah was born rosy, almost nine pounds, and had an APGAR of 9/10. The medical staff joked he would play football for Harvard. When he was removed from my breast for a one-hour check, it was Code Blue. The nurse bellowed into the intercom in a wall and proceeded with CPR. It did not register that *my* child was in trouble. It was like watching a horror film. Next to me, Roger turned white. Another nurse watched him with sharp eyes in case he fainted.

The obstetrician suggested that sudden infant death syndrome was why Jonah stopped breathing. She made evasive comments when we asked questions. At my postpartum checkup she urged me to "not be so sad." She had lost her mother when she was young. I gazed at photographs of her daughters on shelves in her office, and went with her assertions, until a top Boston law firm took us on, on a contingency basis. They turned away ninety-seven percent of inquiries. The experts investigated; a tribunal deemed there was a valid case. The filings and depositions, delayed continually by the obstetrician's defenders, took eight years. Finally we had a court date in 2005.

It was background noise while I played wife, mother, daughter, researcher, associate director. Jonah was the morning star that got drowned out by the sun's rays as the day progressed. I had many other fires to put out, some I created myself. Noah, work, interventions for the chemical sensitivity. My firstborn's narrative lived in me. I cried when I did laundry in the basement of our first house. He used to go there with me when he was in the pouch. I cried when children were abducted in movies, when birth announcements arrived from friends. If the air smelled right or I heard "Have Yourself a Merry Little Christmas," my nose and eyes swelled with despair. The heart of a bereaved mother shattered and not all the pieces went back together. Like Humpty Dumpty.

I wished I had known Barbara when I was pregnant. She coached women on birthing by promoting relaxation and working with the body's rhythms, unlike what I experienced in a conventional hospital, where drugs and harsh interventions were routine. I had, of course, granted consent up front for the hospital to proceed with whatever methods they deemed necessary.

The months before the court date, I worried about going through the proceedings in public. Would I break down in front of strangers? Would I scream at the doctor? We had hopes of winning so she, who, according to our attorney, was sued by five other parties at the time, would have the botchery on her records and perhaps cease to practice. I considered this outcome fairness and public service.

Earlier this year, our lawyer called us in to her office for what I thought was preparation for the trial. Instead we learned that our key expert witness had a stroke and could not testify, and no other doctors would participate in the case. It was a blow. Parents wanted their children's death to mean something. Whatever it was for Jonah and us, it was not going to be determined in court. Roger wanted to find another law firm to pursue it. I pleaded we were already stretched with the MCS, and Noah deserved our attention and resources.

Nothing would bring Jonah back and someone was always missing in our home. Bitterness encircled me like a shark as I treaded not to get bitten. I failed at times. What did one do when she knew someone had gotten away with an act that devastated her life, even when it was not intentional?

I mourned Jonah's upcoming ninth birthday with Barbara on a wintry afternoon.

"He probably didn't feel a lot of pain." She sipped water in her chair.

"How do you know?" I said, sounding defensive. He suffered, I suffered, Roger suffered, Ma suffered ... I recalled lots of suffering. My wee one worked to squeeze through my body with meds in his system. His head was compressed and yanked—

"He lost consciousness quickly," Barbara replied. Her face remained kind.

She was trying to help me. But still. "I wish I did something different for him." I broke down. Even though doctors and therapists assured me it was not my fault, I was not swayed. I let him get hurt.

"Let's do hypnosis around this." Barbara inched toward me in her chair. "Let's see what your intuition says."

I closed my eyes, cleared the thoughts, and got grounded as Barbara counted and soothed with her words. I became one with the black recliner.

"We go higher and higher, to a wise and beautiful place ..."

In my mind, a beam of light shined on a mountaintop, then into darkness. A violet energy filled the space and oscillated.

"Hi, Mommy." A crisp, childlike voice rang in my head, like having a thought.

Jonah?

"How are you?" I cried.

"I'm fine. It's okay, Mommy."

"Are you really there?" Shocked and disbelieving, I latched on the idea of him. "How can I find you?"

"I'm here. When you find peace, you will find me. All you have to do is get connected."

"I'm sorry that you suffered. That awful doctor."

"It's okay, Mommy. She's not worth it."

"Are you cold by yourself in the ground?" It distressed me to know where his body went.

"No, I'm warm and fuzzy."

"Where are you?"

"I'm in your heart, Mommy. I am with you all the time."

"I wish I could give you a hug."

"You can."

In my mind, I saw me holding him, the infant.

"I wish I could see you on earth," I sobbed.

"You can, Mommy. Just look at Noah."

I repeated the silent exchange to Barbara, who suggested I find something tangible to remember the moment by. In came the movie *Contact*, adapted from the Carl Sagan novel, which I had seen a week ago. Jodie Foster's character takes off in an alien-designed capsule to meet extraterrestrials, and ends up talking with her beloved, deceased father at a beach under a sky of giant stars. It is a conversation full of love, all-encompassing vastness, and wonder.

"Will you be there to talk again?" I asked Jonah. "When am I going to be with you?" Some of us had to settle for a momentary, supernatural meeting with our children.

"Yes, anytime. I'm with you. Celebrate my birthday. Play, have fun. Take care of Noah and Daddy."

It felt like the chat was ending, or I could not stay with it. "Wait ..."

"Play, Mommy! Have fun, Mommy!" He was fading.

I heard happy chatters. I said to Barbara, "My kids like to talk, like me, to Roger's dismay. It's great ..."

It got quiet.

"Bye, Jonah. It's really good to know that you are with me. You were a brave and strong child."

"Mommy, you were brave and strong too. On my birthday."

It was like hanging up the phone, knowing the other person would be there to speak another time. Barbara had helped me find a part of me that died with Jonah. No one had treated me this well, given me this kind of care. I was eternally grateful.

Had I made up Jonah to feel better? How could I speak to the spirit of the dead? I was no psychic medium, and neither was Barbara. Yet she believed the connection I had with Jonah always existed. The hypnotherapist helped to set aside the emotional blockages so I could hear him. Jonah was a different consciousness. He saw things at a higher, more inclusive level. He was forgiving, joyous, and full of love. He was not out to get even, like I was.

When I got home, I told Roger about the session. Light glinted from the tears in his eyes. He concurred. "*Just look at Noah* ... Doesn't sound like you. I don't think you made up Jonah."

Our resonance propelled a shift in how I thought of Jonah. I would celebrate instead of grieve him, think of him as upbeat instead of tragic. His birthday became a turning point in my life. I would aim for inner peace so I could talk with him again. It seemed I had access, a portal, to another dimension. My heart eased at the possibility. I didn't need to hold on to the wounding, even though I might revert to sadness at times. The story had changed. I had been put in touch with helpers, people who lightened my burdens. Drs. LaCava and Gordin, the IV nurses, Barbara, and now Jonah.

I was invited to have faith in the Universe.

CHAPTER TWENTY-TWO

"Dr. Gordin says your liver isn't working well?" Barbara leaned back in her chair.

"I told him that although I can relax and sleep better, I still get symptoms from chemicals like cooking gas," I said. We had just returned from my aunt's annual Christmas gathering. It always gave me migraines. Her large gas stove, located next to the common area, was on the whole day. It was a litmus test of how well I really was.

"Dr. Gordin thinks my liver needs help with detoxing and suggested I give myself daily shots of glutathione." I grabbed my upper left arm indicating where the needle would go. "I freaked out. So he said if it made me stressed, not to force it. When I was six, my mother hired a nurse to give me vitamin injections. Every day I watched her stab my thigh with a syringe and felt the pressure of the pink liquid entering my leg." I shivered.

"That sounds awful. Let's talk to your liver," Barbara suggested.

I had talked to my child self, my hands, my deceased son, and had spoken as my mother. Sure, I would chat with my liver.

The aroma of Barbara's mocha latte and our regular Tuesday afternoons comforted me. I settled in the black recliner like a spacewoman ready for takeoff. I patted the blanket on my legs. Part of me was giddy. I was going to talk to an organ. We went through the relaxation routine and set the intention to heal the liver.

"Where are you now?" she asked.

"In my sunny, friendly place," I replied in a low voice.

"Can you see your liver? What does it look like?"

"Steeping in sewage. It's hard and brittle, all stuffed up. It's got crap stuck in it."

"What would you like to do with it?"

An image appeared in my head. "I'd take a sledge hammer and smash it into smithereens. What a piece of junk!" I despised my broken body and its limitations. I wished it a death of some sort.

"No, no, Sue. We are here to heal your body, not to break it. You are your body. *You and your body need each other.*"

True. I only had one liver. If I did not value it, I would not get well. "I'd like the liver to clean out and restore itself."

"Can you come up with a way to help it? Does it need help?"

"I can shine a golden light on it." A flash of warm rays rained on the muddy-brown organ in my mind's eye. "It's changing colors. It's getting burgundy." I marveled at what I was being shown.

"Ex-cellent!"

"It's getting softer and supple ... like it's breathing." I paused to let the makeover take place. A few minutes went by.

"What about the sewage?" Barbara coughed and took a sip of her latte.

"Sewage is turning into a green ocean. The garbage is washing away."

"You are really doing a magnificent job clearing the stagnant bad energy from your liver."

Someone flashed into my head. Should I say something about it? Nah. Today was about my liver.

Barbara cleared her throat. "What is happening?"

"Well, my father's face came up."

"What about your father?"

"When I was young, sometimes he went drinking with my uncles at night and came home rowdy with them." My pulse revved up. "Once at dinnertime my sister and I ran with our rice bowls to hide. She dropped hers and it shattered to pieces. White rice splashed across the gray stone floor. We were scared." Breaking the vessel that held food was a grand no-no in our culture. That and the irrational-acting men frayed the tense psyche that had seen crazy in our house ... *When am I going to stop repeating the narrative of being terrorized?*

"And?" Barbara asked.

"My father's face turned dark pink when he drank. My mother said it was like the color of a pig's liver, that dark red color, like my liver ... I HATE MY LIVER!"

I fell silent.

"Wow," Barbara uttered.

"I had no idea."

"Wow," she repeated.

"My father's drunken face is associated with my liver."

"Maybe you can take back your liver so it's not your father's face."

"Okay. I can't believe it. Just like this? I hate my father so I hate my liver. I have a bad liver and I have chemical sensitivity?" I shifted under the blanket in the recliner.

"Something like that. Everything is related. We are uncovering beliefs that are causing physical symptoms." Barbara waited a few seconds before continuing. "We are born with a body in unity. Everything is supposed to work together. We are a part of something great and perfect."

"What do I do now?" I committed a crime against myself in ignorance. "This has to stop."

"What do you think you should do?"

"Say sorry to my liver?"

"Sounds like a great idea."

I apologized to my liver for the next five minutes. I spoke sorry, thought sorry. Sorry, sorry, sorry. Just a while ago I wanted to destroy it. What was I thinking? I needed this organ. "I continue to shine the healing light on it."

"Good."

"My default has been to get pissed off and blow things apart because I can't deal with it anymore. I get tired of fighting, you know?" I sniffled.

"You're on the right path, Sue. You're determined to heal. Not many people go this far. It's easier to go to your default—anger—than to face the trauma imprints and heal them."

"I don't have role models who change beliefs or handle frustrations. I'm lucky that you are here."

I paused.

"For the next week, apologize to your liver every day when you wake up. Ask it to help you cleanse your body. How's the liver now? Are you still shining the light on it?"

"Yes, and the liver is getting strong and soft. It's chugging along," I said with a smile. "Like the hinds of a racehorse. It's powerful, ready to go. I am a horse in the Chinese zodiac."

"Great!"

Barbara helped me out of my trance. When I opened my eyes, her grin came to view.

"No needles for me, whew! I only have to change how I think of the liver subconsciously. My body is my friend. It's really that simple? How cool is that?" I said.

"Everything can be healed." She implored. "We need to change the deep-seated ideas that get us sick in the first place. It's interesting how the mind and body dance with each other. Have you heard of Caroline Myss? She's a medical intuitive. You'd like her book *Anatomy of the Spirit*. She writes about why people get sick on an energetic level."

I'd never heard of her and was happy to learn other insight on wellness. "I'll look up the book."

I left Barbara's office, still stunned about my liver. What other organs were connected to my angst? The brain? Like the loss of balance symbolized how I was not supported as a child?

The body sent messages. How would I decipher them? I craved to know the meaning of my symptoms, the relationship between the mind and body, how traumas and emotional issues manifested in the body. Then I could address the root causes of my issues.

Maybe when I finished with Barbara I would feel even better than before I developed MCS? My intuition said it was possible. An engine in me ignited. I felt greedy. I wanted a liberated, stronger version of me.

CHAPTER TWENTY-THREE

The vinyl seat under me was soft and tight, like my insides. It was a long trip to the gastroenterologist's office in Mount Auburn Hospital, which required stressful driving through Cambridge. I dreaded the appointment and wondered if I should talk to my intestines next. I was only thirty-nine but my paternal family had a history of colon cancer.

Three years ago, the GI had found a small polyp and ordered me to return.

"When I had my first colonoscopy, I threw up on the way home," I said to Dr. Chobanian.

"I'm sorry to hear about the vomiting. Are you sensitive to narcotics?" he asked.

Yes, to all meds. "Would you help me deal with that this time?" I had given up mentioning issues like MCS or mercury preservatives in drugs to medical personnel. It invited weird looks and no resolution. The same happened when I told the server at a restaurant that I was allergic to sugar.

"We can hold off on the Versed and control the amount of Fentanyl." Tall, in round-rimmed glasses and a white coat, Dr. Chobanian reminded me of a snowy owl.

"What is Versed?" I queried across his glass-covered desk. Before my first colonoscopy, I did not know to ask questions.

The GI explained it was a sedative, a "happy drug," to calm people before getting anesthesia. It sounded like the medication that made snapping sounds in my head before the vein surgery. Strange how people needed to get jolly before going under. How we built up anxiety before giving up total control of ourselves, and how modern medicine kept patients compliant.

"What if I have other ways to relax before the procedure?" I asked.

"You don't have to have the Versed," he replied with a grin.

"I'm willing to tolerate pain. Is it possible to skip the painkiller too?"

"No. I don't think that would be comfortable."

"It's not general anesthesia, right?" Questioning an authority figure went against my grain. But my body, like everything else I own, was my responsibility and deserved respect. MCS had been teaching me this lesson.

"Fentanyl is not an anesthetic. It's a narcotic. We pump a lot of air into your large intestine to blow it up and check the surfaces for abnormalities. The air would make it painful if you don't get the Fentanyl."

"I'm willing to bear the pain if you can give me the least amount of medication. I'm chemically sensitive." I changed my mind about expounding on MCS since this doctor was responsive.

"Sure. Sure. I can control the amount of drugs and start with a small amount."

"Thank you. I see a hypnotherapist. I'll practice self-hypnosis for this."

"I was a psychology major in college. I am intrigued by this. Sure. Sure. We can start with very little and go from there."

Last time he said "sure, sure" we met about the first colonoscopy. From my chart he announced I was "young and healthy." Still dealing with acute MCS symptoms then, I felt like fresh meat, a veal going to the slaughterhouse. This time, I shook-squeezed the doctor's hand with some confidence that the outcome would be different. I so appreciated his willingness to accommodate me. Whether my body would cooperate during and after the procedure, I did not know.

~

Three weeks later I was in Mount Auburn for the procedure. On a gigantic monitor next to a keyboard and medical instruments, the screen displayed shiny, pink, curvy surfaces. The camera traversed the organ as if it were driving through a tunnel.

"That's my intestine?" Versed-less, I felt upbeat anyway. I was all right from emptying the gut after drinking a natural solution the GI prescribed. We were near the end of the invasive process.

"Yes. Looks pretty good so far." The doctor's booming voice filled the cold, sterile air. A pump hissed near him as he directed a tube in my abdomen. I pictured being blown up for Macy's Thanksgiving Parade. The IV on the back of my hand ached a little. I was used to that. As promised, the doctor had injected a small amount of painkiller. There was some cramping and bloating, but I managed.

I tried to watch the show on the wall—my nearsightedness only gave blurred action. Touching my right index finger to the thumb, I drifted and fell into an alternate consciousness.

The large intestine is about five feet long ... The colon belongs to the second chakra, associated with the color orange, according to Caroline Myss. The energy center embodies power relationship with others, creativity, finances, and elimination. Most of my relatives worried about money and power ... Ungon (grandfather) was a stamp carver, a self-taught poet, and had sixteen children. He was artistic. He died of malaria when my father was five ... Ba was the youngest. His older brother scolded and beat him, told him when he ate enough. Ba and Ma were children during World War II ... grew up in harsh situations, poverty ... I'm creative too. Roger and I've struggled with finances since the MCS started ... Little Shogi had no power, like Ba and Ma. The adult Sue does. She is an associate director, helping to run a department ... That's external power. I spoke up to this doctor about my need for the least drugs. That's internal power ...

More cramps sent me back to the exam room. I would not ask Dr. Chobanian for more painkiller. The memory of Barbara counting backwards and the little me visiting a sunny, warm, flowers-swaying field appeared in my head. Young Sue-Yi was there to dance, a red balloon tied to her wrist.

"Everything looks great. No polyps this time. I will see you in the recovery area." Under a light green mask and cap, Dr. Chobanian towered over me.

Good. I pressed a blue button in my mind, a device I had concocted with Barbara. I envisioned letting out all the meds from my body to help my liver detox, like dropping bombs from a B-52. After the bombs were gone, I switched on the gold button and surrounded myself, especially the liver, in golden light.

A nurse pushed me to an open area and pulled the mauve curtain shut for privacy. "Dr. Chobanian will be with you in fifteen minutes. How are you feeling?"

I checked my head and stomach. A little hungry, no nausea. "Not bad."

Roger's baseball-capped head popped inside the curtain. "Feeling okay? The doctor said it went well."

"Yes, I only need to eat and sleep. This feels much better than last time." I recalled puking in the car and feeling ill for a week. "I don't think I'll need the vitamin C IV later." I had scheduled a session in case the self-hypnosis–liver detox team needed backup.

"That's great, Sue." Roger sat in the chair next to my head and held my hand.

"Thanks for all your support. I think I am getting better from the MCS!"

"It's about time."

In my semi-daze an idea popped up. If my body could endure the colonoscopy, maybe I could handle a mega-long flight to Taiwan? It had been twenty years since I visited Asia. Barbara and my excavation of the past made it real again. There were people I did not dare to miss. Like my maternal aunt, Dua-Yi, the island of sanity in young Shogi's ocean of fear. She was eighty, getting old. I could still cry about leaving her at the drop of a hat.

Perhaps it was time to reclaim pieces of me that were trapped in time and locality. And perhaps it was time to see my father in nearby Hong Kong. It had been six years since I had seen him. The last real communication we had was before his stroke.

CHAPTER TWENTY-FOUR

I might as well take the racing heart out of my chest and hold it still.

The anticipation of seeing Ba jolted me from the exhaustion of a sixteen-hour flight.

"Noah, make sure you have all your things." I held his hand, dragged a suitcase behind me, and walked in sync with Roger leaving Baggage Claim. I was glad to finish the journey from Boston to Hong Kong, our first leg to Asia. It was February 7, 2008, the Lunar New Year, which explained why our enormous Boeing 777 had ten passengers. Before getting on the plane, I worried about the effects of germicides sprayed in cabins, lack of fresh air, and getting enough rest. All that went out the window when I considered my father.

The cavernous Hong Kong International Airport terminal bustled with dark-haired East Asians, people who looked like me. It would not be as easy to single out my father in the crowd here. What would he look like after a stroke two years ago? I had imagined different versions: in a wheel chair with a dangling hand, limping with a cane, or drooling. When I heard of his ailment, I recalled a nightmare of my causing him to bleed in the brain. I might have picked up his vibe. Ba did not share his news—a cousin e-mailed—and it did not compel me to fly across the globe to see him. I was in the midst of battling serious MCS and did not feel charitable. My sister Lily was in the vicinity and did the honor.

Deeper down, my remorse about my detachment, along with Ba's liver face, lurked in my psyche. What was I doing? I wanted to resolve all the ills in my life and have everything squared away. Did life work that way? I did not *have to* see my father. But I did. He was my son's grandfather and I was his daughter.

It took a bit to get used to being in Asia. I was used to seeing mostly Caucasians from my twenty-eight years of living in the northeast United States. Around me, signs in Mandarin and English with red and gold firecracker motifs hung high in the airport concourse. A tinge of joy seeped into my chest. It was the best time to be in China or Taiwan. The New Year painted cheer on everyone.

"Shogi. Roger." Ba stood by the gate in a beige cap jacket, and khakis. His eyes dashed at me, Roger, and quickly to Noah. Roger shook his hand.

"How was your flight, Noah?" Ba's grin, very similar to mine, shined on our ten-year-old.

"Good." Noah looked up. "We had free ramen on the plane. I had two cups."

"Say '*Ungon*,' Noah. Be polite." I put my hand on his shoulder.

Our son complied, earning a pat on the head from Ba.

My father pulled out not one but three little packets from inside of his jacket and gave each of us one. "A red envelope for you. Happy New Year," he said.

"Ba, *sieh-sieh*. You didn't need to give us adults a present." The tradition was, once children were income earning, they gifted the parents. "I didn't bring a red envelope for you." I brought him wool socks and hand warmers from America.

"Don't worry about it. Small treat." He gazed at me and turned quickly. "We should catch the subway to your hotel before the fireworks. Otherwise there will be a lot of people on it after it's over." He started toward a booth to buy tickets for our ride.

That was when I noticed his off-balanced gait. Tears swelled in my eyes, for I knew that Ba had to manage alone while he convalesced. In my memory, my father was a tall, strong person who smacked and cursed. Now in his late sixties, his face wrinkled, he leaned toward one side when he walked. He had limited funds but he gifted us red envelopes for the holiday. His vulnerability touched me in bewildering ways. He was not quite the demon I had built him up to be. How we thought the worst of people when we were angry with them. Walking behind Ba, I wiped a tear by letting go of Noah's hand and regrabbed it.

Like a hospital, the airport was a place of life and death for me. I would say hello and farewell to loved ones, not knowing how much time I had with them, if I would ever see them again. This was how it was between Ba and me. He commuted to work across cities and continents. I moved away.

We were in the honeymoon phase of our reunion. When we were young he traveled too. We greeted his return with delight, and naiveté caused us to anticipate benevolence. Ba was a landmine of irate nitpicking. His discontent festered if he stayed home too long. It was a relief for everyone when he returned to the road. As a child, I covered up each inflicted wound with a scar. Now I had a jittery heart wrapped in thick skin.

I had helped my mother collect more than half of their assets from the divorce. My siblings and I felt it was only fair for the abuse she endured. Ba left the United States with contempt and later suffered a stroke. I wondered if he would bring up the uneven distribution of their property, and what I would say to that.

In the subway tunnels, my father zipped through the walkway between stations. He seemed to be doing better than I expected. I chased behind him, bags and Noah in tow. Maybe he was as uncomfortable as I was about seeing each other. I sighed and turned to see where Roger was. He had stopped at various places to take pictures. He, like Noah, had never set foot in Asia.

~

After leaving our bags at the hotel, we strolled and stopped at a restaurant Ba suggested. He had lived here for over a decade and knew his way around. It was full of people during the New Year. Plates clanged and chopsticks clicked around me. Eaters gabbed and slurped in loud, celebratory style.

"Noah would like noodle soup. He 's allergic to shrimp. I'll ask if there is any in this broth," I said to my family and put down the menu. One never knew exactly what went in a dish in a Chinese establishment. I doubted the cook would care whether his fare caused hives in patrons—we were not in America anymore—but asking would be an attempt to quell my anxiety about Noah's allergies.

Roger and I ordered our Chinese-American staple, stir-fried chicken with vegetables and rice, a shame because we were in the land of Real Chinese Food. I was not the adventurous foodie in my birth family. Lily was. She was wedding banquet worthy, someone who enjoyed the abundant quantity and variety of dishes. Chicken feet, abalone, fried fish head, pork ears were welcomed by her palate.

Ba sat next to me. We chatted about his life in Hong Kong, Noah's routine, and danced around the elephant in the room—his divorce. Two years ago, I had replied to his e-mail complaint asking why we did not seek him out, and I conveyed what his temper and violence had done to our family. It was my first time expressing dismay and wrath on the subject. After that he disappeared. Months later I heard the news of his apoplexy.

"Noah, how's the soup?" Ba asked across our small table.

"Good."

"Looks yummy, Noah." I eyed his bowl and got the chopsticks going in mine. It was surreal. I had been in Hong Kong when I was three. Ma, Lily, and I stopped here en route to Saigon, to join my father who worked in air logistics support during the Vietnam War. We returned to Taiwan after three months because my mother got scared. Later Ba rationalized we went there "to play" like tourists.

"How's your food, Rog?" I asked.

"Pretty good."

Great. My family was happily fed. Back to the ping-pong of do-I-address-what-happened with my father.

"Ba, you've worked and lived in Hong Kong a long time now. Are you thinking of staying here?" I said.

"Maybe. I am going to see if I can make some money in China." He rested his chopsticks on his rice bowl.

"That's good. Are you managing okay the symptoms from the stroke?" Raised to not make eye contact to show respect, I looked his long fingers. They looked like mine.

"I get dizzy and lose balance. I see doctors for medicine. I am trying a new drug. Maybe that'll help more. I try to go hiking." He picked up some bok choy with his chopsticks.

Strange, we both lost balance. "Be careful when you hike. You walked faster than me in the subway." Secretly I was glad he did not need more help.

"Do you think it was fair your mother took both houses?" he blurted out.

It was as if I ate a bird and it got stuck in my throat. Goosebumps spread from my core to the limbs. Just like how it used to be when I got in trouble with him. I did not know what to say. Defend my mother? I would have to drag out our family history in public. Stand up to my father? I did not dare. All the maneuvering around my parents' divorce, taking care of my mother instead of him, and the meeting now, in a way, was my passive aggression toward him. While I fought him back in hypnosis, I remained a wimp in person.

After some pause, I grumbled, "Yeah. It was fair."

He looked away in disgust. His face was far from the burgundy hue in my inner child's eye.

Ba's annoyance still cut into me, but there was nothing else to say. I came to pay respect on my way to Taiwan. It was not my plan to challenge him. Just seeing him walking and standing was enough. I understood that he suffered because of his tough childhood and alienation from the family he created. The image of him plodding alone in the subway underpass was inked in my mind. It broke my heart. I loved him but could not be close to him. Even though he left distressing imprints on me, my grievance was no longer with the man who made the effort to eat by my side. I would deal with the father in my memory in a trance, in the safety of the black recliner.

CHAPTER TWENTY-FIVE

I never thought I could curse and argue in English with a Caucasian husband in my hometown—Tainan, Taiwan. Under the midday sun, my hands flew.

"I tried to address your issues. The stained pillow at my cousin's place, the Internet access, people assuming you eat beef. Now I shouldn't translate the menu for you?" Two doors away, we left Noah, Ma, who joined us on this leg of the trip, and my cousin Ling-Ling in the middle of lunch.

"I asked what they had!" he scoffed. "I didn't ask you to translate the menu."

"We go eat and I automatically do it for you. There were thirty items and I weed out the stuff you don't like. I was telling the waitress to have the wok washed before cooking Noah's food. You know he had a bad reaction in Hong Kong." Shellfish was everywhere in Asia. It was

213

hard to see Noah's head dozing on a banquet table from the side effects of Benadryl.

"If you listen to my preferences, what I want—"

"No pork ginger pepper Chinese vegetables," I snapped. My eyes threw a dagger at a gawker-by. "You needed help ordering but chided me in front of everyone." I was speaking two languages to three parties. I got flustered.

"Just because I came with you doesn't mean I gave up my right to have preferences." Roger ripped off his blue cap.

"Rights again." I made quotes in the air. I came to see my homeland, to heal. Not this. Roger's comfort was on my mind ever since we landed in Taiwan. Nothing seemed okay for him. My relatives' enthusiasm for feeding him grated on his nerves. After facing my father, I thought I was home free. I expected Roger to be his adaptable self—he had an adventurous spirit and had lived abroad before. Instead, we fought every day.

"We don't have time to debate. People are waiting," I urged.

"Why did you ask me to come if you don't want to deal with me?" He whipped his hat back over his head. "You want me to smile standing next to you the whole time?"

"I've tried to deal with you. Just not with full attention. I wanted you here because I got better from the chemical sensitivity and can travel to see ... to share my family and memories with you." I broke down and made out distorted Chinese characters on surrounding signs.

"That's why I came, but you are not considering my feelings."

"Maybe I am not as thoughtful as you want me to be. I've got a lot to revisit ... I want to close the loop."

"Nice for you. It's all about you. You got sick, you do this, you do that, you're getting better. You. You. You!" he said, pointing. "I can't do this anymore. I have already been to Hong Kong to see your father."

"That wasn't so terrible."

Roger pulled at the brim of his hat. "I was worried if you were going be okay seeing him."

"That was nice of you." A surprise to me, given how he was reacting now. "Rog, this trip is fourteen days, twelve days if you subtract the flying. In three days we'll be in Taipei and on our own. Can you go along for a few more days?"

"I have gone along for a week, and you don't want to talk to me when I need to—"

"Dammit! Aren't we talking now?" I shrieked. In public, in the land that taught me it was shameful. "Just not for hours at a time! I offered to buy a pillow for you but you refused it. I'm here instead of with my cousin back there. I have limited time." I hated that fatalistic feeling of now or never. "I have gone to every one of *your* family's events for at least twelve years. I even converted to Judaism. You can't suck it up for twelve days?"

"Fuck you, Sue. I am done. I am leaving for Taipei tomorrow. I'll check into the hotel early."

"Fine!" At the corner of my eye, I spotted Ling-Ling, Noah, and Ma exiting the restaurant, plastic containers in their hands.

~

It was a good thing my cousin had taken us to Jhongyi Elementary School before the spat. My old school appeared nothing like it was twenty-six years ago, except for the wide banyan trees with long whiskers hanging from their branches. I loved sitting in the shade of these giants, being sheltered from the boiling subtropical heat. Like Ling-Ling's mother, my Dua-Yi, they were still there, always there.

Noah, Roger, and I sauntered the hallways. The school was empty during the New Year.

"Mommy's elementary school. What do you think?" I said to our son.

"Goo-ood." He peered through a glass wall that made the entire classroom visible. Rows of wooden tables stood at attention before a blank blackboard.

"It's different than your school in America, where you sit in a circle with your teacher. There is no privacy here because of the glass wall," I said. In childhood, when we napped after lunch in school, we had to turn our heads away from the corridors because each class got graded on uniformity and silence.

"I'm going to Amah by the jungle gym," Noah said and ran off.

"These desks are so small." I turned to Roger. "They used to feel as big as I was, but here they are ... tiny."

He put an arm around me. "You grew but the tables did not."

I surveyed the room. Things had moved on. The floor was covered in vinyl laminate instead of cement and dirt. Here, I memorized numerous Mandarin characters stroke by stroke. I learned multiplication. Teacher Chen whipped our hands, and we swept the floors with straw brooms. I ate from a stainless-steel lunch box that Ma packed. A brined egg, rice, and stir-fried cabbage were steamed hot at the school. Here, I borrowed my first book from the library. Friends taught me how to pump a swing.

It was not all bad.

The energy of the old traumas, mostly confronted in the black recliner, was dissipating. I was no longer a child, and corporal punishment in Taiwanese schools was outlawed in 2007. At five foot six, I probably overshadowed Teacher Chen.

It was a day of aha's. Earlier we jogged by an older couple dancing under trees. Their friends played guitar and drums near them. Smiles radiated from all faces. Unlike what I remembered, there was pleasure in the Taiwanese consciousness. It was okay to enjoy life. Growing up I sensed those around me carried backbreaking weight simply because they existed. It was disloyal to show cheer. Ma said I acted "like every day is New Year's Eve." I internalized the sorrow and projected it, believing every Taiwanese had a miserable life due to a history of mean teachers, Japanese occupation, World War II, and marshal law. I held the pain as inheritance, a badge of honor. Maybe this way I would be like everyone else; I would not suffer alone.

Roger and I negotiated that he stay in Tainan for one more day so we could celebrate Noah's tenth birthday with relatives. We would leave together and shorten our visit in the southern city by a day. It surprised my aunt and shredded my core.

The morning of our departure, frigid air under thick clouds filled the narrow alleyway at Ling-Ling's. We huddled in a circle to say good-bye.

"Dua-Yi, you take care." I put my arm into hers. This was it.

"*Herh, herh.*" Her milky brown eyes, dimmed by glaucoma, glanced at me through thick glasses. Paper-thin eyelids half covered her once direct gaze.

"Thanks for everything you have done for me, my family. I—" My face flushed, the weeping spigots about to blow.

"I know. I know," she replied. My aunt understood me telepathically. It was always like that, a visceral sense of each other. "*You grew up here*," she added.

Those words sent my tears gushing. She was my home, my anchor. I did not have that kind of connection with Ma, who was spent by her ire at my father and life.

My aunt patted my shoulder while leaning on a cane. "Shogi, come again. Your son very funny, cute." She gurgled her hearty laugh. *Heh, heh, heh* ... Noah had imitated her tortoise-like walk with the cane during his birthday party. Dua-Yi laughed the hardest.

It was the voice that calmed Shogi's soul, a lifesaver in the explode-anytime family atmosphere. I trusted her. My mother, who did not trust herself, looked to her eldest sister on big decisions. Dua-Yi tried to shield my mother from Ba's smiting hands and helped her raise three kids. She was strict with her own children, but she showered us young ones with kindness. She made me dresses, rice sack toys, unlimited fried pork loins, and sang children's songs. When I was twelve, Lily and I were left with her for a year while my parents settled in the United States.

Now the gray, osteoporosis-stricken version of my aunt hunched next to me and Ling-Ling, who would drive us to the train station. I had planned to break down like Dua-Yi had done privately before, wailing "When will we be together again?" But she did not get excited. I gathered that she was too old to get riled up. All I could do was wish her health and longevity. I promised to call her from America.

My inner child bid Dua-Yi farewell once more, probably for life. We climbed in the car and waved. I hung my head low in the backseat while Ling-Ling made small talk: When do you go back to work after you get home? When does Noah return to school? Is it cold in Massachusetts? I wiped my face with coat sleeves and tried to answer each question. Everyone ignored my sobs, including me. I had condensed my time with my crumbling aunt to appease a spouse.

At the train station, I hugged Ling-Ling, who had retired from teaching high school English. She was able to communicate with Roger fully by the end of our stay. Hosting us was so exhausting that she fell asleep after stopping at a red light. We invited her to visit us.

The high-speed rail glided into the terminal to take us to Taiwan's capital, Taipei. The technological marvel briefly shut off my waterworks. I blurted out to no one, "We should have this in America."

Inside the mint-condition coach, Roger, Noah, and I settled into a row of three seats. Noah put a stuffed animal on the windowsill next to him. It was a parting gift from another cousin. After a chime, my hometown Tainan slid away in full force. The old feeling of Ba taking us away from the city known for Dua-Yi and evening walks near her house crept up.

I was leaving again.

The rail stopped in Taichung, where I lived when I was four. Ba told me I often had asked to ride the train to return to my aunt. In the aisle, passengers walked by and stared at Noah, then Roger and me. They seemed curious about the looks of a mixed-race child and his parents. An uncle said our bespectacled son looked like Ha-Lee-Poh-Tuh, Harry Potter, which earned delighted nods from the clan.

The train picked up speed. It was the first unscheduled moment I was not pleading or fighting with Roger. I could not bring myself to talk to him. I wondered who I married, who I was—*not* the subservient wife who married a foreigner. Roger and I walked together for fifteen years, and we were partners. He was supportive of my pursuit for health once he saw the benefits. He knew my history and attachments, and chose to whittle down precious time here with protracted, fierce arguments. Maybe the immersion in a foreign land this time sent him over the edge.

Having to choose between Dua-Yi and Roger left me unraveled. Would my body assert again to show the mind's unrest? Despite the jetlag, quarrels, changes in food and environment, I did not feel sick. I kept my eyes fixed outside the train as the landscape flew by, frame by frame. Gone were tiles of emerald rice paddies along the train tracks, now replaced by random shoots of buildings, houses, telephone poles, and occasional red Buddhist temples under golden roofs. I drank in the images and my salty tears.

CHAPTER TWENTY-SIX

"I am sorry, Sue." Roger's eyes focused on mine. The wooden arms of his chair creaked.

I stared straight at him, then Barbara next to me. "Hmm," was all I could muster.

The events in Taiwan raged between us like wildfire since we got home. I asked for the meeting with Barbara because I worried about the hours of weeping and poor sleep I logged since the trip. Our arguments cycled endlessly between my resentment about leaving Dua-Yi early and Roger's anger for not being heard while there.

Barbara turned to Roger. "It might be helpful for Sue to hear why you are sorry."

"I'm sorry because I was demanding in Tainan and did not consider your feelings," he stated in a crisp voice.

I would have loved to hear this at the time or a week ago. *He's apologizing to save face.* "That's nice," I announced, not quite meaning it.

"It sounds like he's sincere." Barbara straightened her blue cardigan and looked toward me.

I knew Barbara was my therapist. She said to come in, and if she thought we needed marriage counseling, she would make a referral. At the moment it appeared she was on Roger's side, explaining for him, which set off a fire in my gut.

"He sounds sincere now," I said, "but he's never apologized before this appointment. I realize that I have been sick, difficult, out of commission, using a lot of money with the MCS, and then this trip ..." Damn. I cried. I lose.

My hands clenched the arms of the black recliner. I said to Roger, "You couldn't be nice for twelve days? Have you been holding things in until I feel better?"

"I was trying to tell you that I was uncomfortable at your cousin's house. You did not want to listen to me." Roger adjusted his glasses.

"I listened. Just not for hours."

Barbara cut in. "Sue, I understand you are mad that the trip was not what you wished for. Often men don't want to feel. Your husband is telling you *what he feels.*"

I wanted to nail Barbara to the wall with my eyes. "So? He told me I was not listening to him. Not true."

"Sue." Barbara dropped my name like a lead ball. "He said he was sorry. Did you hear it?"

Her tone shocked me out of crying. She never talked to me that way. I glanced at Roger. He wore a tweed jacket and shirt, hiding behind his lawyer persona. His calmness irked me.

"I heard. I don't trust him. He's just saying it in front of you, so he looks okay in public," I said. I was sure of this.

Barbara pulled close her cardigan. "That's not how I see it," she said. "When you fight with each other, your trauma imprints get triggered and both of you regress to your two-year-old, no, six-month-old selves. Perhaps in front of me, you are reminded to hold both your adult and inner child selves together. I think that's what Roger is doing. He was not happy about what happened and he acted badly. He apologizes."

Indeed we stabbed each other with words and scorn, and brawled for survival in blood and gore. It was cruel to our relationship.

"I mean what I said, Sue. I am sorry." Roger leaned toward me.

"Are you holding against me the chemical sensitivity, the cost, the trip, this therapy?" I asked.

"I am not holding a grudge. I love you. I want us to move on. I know it hasn't been easy for you."

"That's a nice thing to say, Roger." Barbara's eyes twinkled.

"I don't know." I stared at my black boots.

Barbara rested her arms on her lap. "Why do you think you are hanging on to Roger's mistake in Taiwan?"

"Because he knew Dua-Yi meant a lot to me and still cut short my time with her. My father did this. Moved us away from her several times." My inner child spoke, the adult me thought Roger and I *would* watch each other's backs. "I felt betrayed. I have to be on guard." I pulled my engagement and wedding rings on and off my finger.

"And being angry?" Barbara asked. "Does anger serve a purpose here?"

"Yes. Because I don't want to be hurt again."

"You use anger as protection?"

"I guess."

"That takes a lot of energy," she said.

"I guess."

"Maybe if you feel safe you wouldn't need to be angry."

"That would be lovely."

"Would you feel safer if I point out that Roger has been on your side and he apologized when he made a mistake? *Roger is not your father.*"

Stunned, I looked at my husband. I turned back at Barbara. My ears turned hot. "He is not my father," I said. It was true that he was on my side. Time after time Roger showed up during and after a crisis. My father stayed away.

As if Barbara pulled off a cloth from my husband's head and torso, I saw the man I chose to be with, not his wounded inner child. He got to have his issues too.

I covered my face. "I'm sorry. I have a long memory. I've been holding on to being wronged. Again." My fingertips pushed tears away from my eyes. "I am sorry, Rog."

Barbara smiled. "When you change a belief, a weight comes off."

"I do feel lighter," I said.

"Perhaps you won't need to be on guard anymore. You are no longer a helpless child. You can assert for yourself now." Barbara beamed.

I sensed the warmth in the room. I had a chance to speak my mind in a neutral place and appreciated Roger and Barbara taking the time. They both showed me I was worthy of it. I was relieved my husband did not hold the MCS ordeal against me. It was the kind of safety I did not have as a child.

"I love you too." I caught up to Roger's declaration.

We thanked Barbara for the session. Outside, he opened the car door for me.

"That was helpful," he said. "I know it's probably not a good time to bring it up, but how long do you think you'll need to see Barbara?"

It wasn't a good time, but a reasonable question. "I don't know ... I'm close. There is something to figure out about being vulnerable and on guard." I want to finish the job. "I need a little longer with Barbara."

That night, I wrote in my journal:

I hated choosing between Roger, my Present, over Dua-Yi, my Past. It broke my heart. Maybe I didn't need to consider it as an either-or. Maybe I get to keep both in different formats. Roger in the physical and my aunt in my heart. It's like having Noah and Jonah in my life.

Living with this chemical sensitivity is a lot and Roger has met the challenges thus far, sometimes not so willingly, but he is human. I thought losing Jonah and the MCS would tear us apart, but we have been all right. I can't take that for granted. Roger is a good man.

Before getting sick, I was already exhausted. I didn't ask for help or a respite. I didn't know how. The MCS enabled me to demand things. I got Roger's devotion, my mother's cooking, Noah to grow up faster, and an excuse not to deal with my father. What a way to gain assistance and opt out! Illness is no fun, though. I had to get really, awfully sick to have my needs met. Being sick served a purpose for me. Oh my.

I was the eldest child who had to be trouble-free. My mother was always preoccupied. The only time I got her complete attention was when I was hot with a fever. She'd buy a fresh coconut, slice off its top, and insert a straw. She told me the juice would bring down my temperature. I saw her large eyes burning with concern for me.

I learned that I am important only when I am sick.

CHAPTER TWENTY-SEVEN

Just when things settled down with Roger, I was offered something else to realign before I graduated from MCS school. My sister's trouble was the iceberg I had hoped to avoid. But here it was, illuminated on the laptop: an e-mail saying she was at a hospital in Thailand having an MRI for her back. The doctor recommended surgery. It would cost over five thousand American dollars and she could not imagine how much more it would cost in the United States. "Anyway, don't tell mother yet. She would freak out like usual ... I'll let you know if I decide to go through with it."

I sank my face in my hands. *Do I get involved?* A dinner of dumplings with scallion sauce became heavy dough in my stomach. Any predicament involving my family of origin was a trigger. We shared a past, ways of reacting. Lily's message would set off a series of events that would take a lot of energy. Don't tell mother yet. Sure. We were extensions of Ma. There was no cutoff of where she ended and where her children began. We existed in sickness and in crisis.

My sister left Los Angeles almost two years ago to teach in Singapore. In previous missives I had encouraged her to explore online her next move, relax to ease her back pain. Yet her condition worsened, there was no next job, and she had nowhere to go but toward our mother. Lily's return to the states was a piano waiting to drop on me.

I felt for Lily. I knew her back was bothersome—but what prompted her to go to a hospital in Thailand? I pushed off the desk and walked toward the window. Another gray April day. Piles of soiled ice from a long winter had settled along the street, a six-month stain that returned every year. Like my birth family's neediness, it never really went away.

An open back operation seemed severe. Was it necessary? With Lily's permission, I quickly forwarded her MRI to a doctor who specialized in pain management. I called my sister the next day, explored possibilities, including sending our mother to help her. She decided to hold off on the surgery.

My sister was barely two years younger than me but I felt much older. When she was three she fell down a flight of concrete stairs riding a tricycle. Preoccupied with our measles-stricken baby brother, Ma lost track of us. I was the one who alerted her that a neighbor had carried Lily to the hospital. She ended up with three scars above her eyes. Blindness was avoided, but the trauma fused her to our mother and, to some extent, me. My sister had won awards for speech, science, and photojournalism. In a crisis, she remained a fellow face-slap sufferer at the hands of our father.

Lily could not deal with Ma's reaction on her health dilemma, so I volunteered to relay it. I descended to my mother's room at the other end of the house. Crossing a big room to reach her, I bit my lips. There was no way to sweeten the news.

"Ma, I just talked to Lily." I leaned on the doorway and met her eyes next to a dim floor lamp. "Her back really hurts and she went to Thailand to see if she could get cheap surgery."

Ma turned off CNN with a remote and pulled her legs off a small ottoman. "Ah-yah. Lily. Never smooth." Her shoulders hunched forward. "Back surgery. Bad."

"She may not need it. Some spine adjustment and getting stronger would help," I said.

"Lily need job with health insurance back here. Then operation."

My mother wished Lily stayed in her condo in L.A. and kept the job with the nice salary at a newspaper. "Lily no return California. No money to pay mortgage." Ma looked up from her plaid chair.

Roger and I had a half-a-million-dollar mortgage. My sister was collecting rent from her condo.

"Can she come home early? Her back hurt now," my mother said.

"What do you mean *home?*" I had seen this word in my sister's e-mails too, as in "can't wait to come home."

"Home, America." My mother's gaze swam around my face. "*Here.* You kids take care each other."

"You mean *I* take care of Lily. It's never the other way around. She doesn't think ahead." Lily was my maid of honor who frowned when asked to help with the wedding dress.

"She in trouble." Ma's eyes reddened. "Lily need help."

Ma's distress pierced through my firewall facade. I was concerned too. But being a designated helper plunged me into a mental frying pan.

"Lily is almost forty. Why are you using me to take care of her?"

"Here I help you with Noah." Ma zinged me like lightning.

It was a different interpretation of intentions. I offered my mother residence so she would feel safe about leaving Ba. By the time she moved in, I was sick with MCS. Ma viewed the arrangement as her supporting me so I could recover, work, and raise a child. What she did not realize was that I had become her letter writer, stylist, doctor finder, bill inquirer, and fighter over bad car repairs.

And now, Lily's aide.

"You kids help each other." Ma wiped her face and nose with the back of her hand.

Ten years ago, Lily and I got into an argument in front of my parents. Ma and Ba, being ninth and sixteenth in birth order, respectively, said the usual—I was older and should accommodate Lily. For once I did not. My mother went into shock and lost her short-term memory. The ER doctor said, "Whatever you did, don't do it again."

No room for Shogi to object. Currently my sister's bad back trumped everything. I was powerless in my mother's powerlessness. My head took a spin. Our gas furnace was around the corner. I tried to stay away from it and had been okay since working with Barbara. Time for the relaxation tape. I had phased out the IVs two years ago and really did not want to resume them.

I blinked and refocused on Ma. "I'll talk to Roger about Lily's stay. But it'll be temporary, a month. Until Lily settles and figures out where she wants to live. I am not taking care of Lily like Dua-Yi took care of you. She has options." My sister had saved money while she worked in Asia. Maybe she could rent a place near us.

"*Herh-la. Sieh-sieh.*" Ma turned away from me and put CNN back on.

I ran upstairs. *What did I agree to do?* I was thankful to find the door to the office open. Roger glanced at me from the laptop. "What's going on?" he said.

"I know my mother is already living here," I leaned on the wall across from him. "Lily needs a place to stay too. Her back is very bad. Ma wants to give Lily her room. She proposed to sleep on the floor in the next room."

"You were nervous that your sister would end up here. Now she's coming."

"This is why I can't relax—I'm constantly on the hook." I sat and rested my head on the loveseat across from Roger's desk. "I'm really sorry. This is a huge imposition. Ma's very worried about her. I'm conflicted about helping because I think Lily could have found a job or an apartment earlier."

"Let's do the right thing, Sue. She needs help so we'll help her." Roger pulled at his khaki cap. "It's not going to be long term. Lily should have a plan about what she's going to do."

"Thank you, Rog. One month, I told my mother. I know she will be grateful to you." I stood up to hug him. "I love you for your decency. I always have."

CHAPTER TWENTY-EIGHT

The following week, I was back in the black recliner rubbing my forehead. "I got dizzy again. I'm feeling invaded. My sister has a serious back issue and is coming to stay with us."

"Oh dear." Barbara reached for her water bottle. "What does Roger say about this?"

"He understands, and says Lily should have a timeline—a month is okay. He even suggests we clear out the ground level so Lily and my mother can have the whole floor."

"That's generous of him."

"He's really helping on this one. I'd like for Lily to work with you on the cause of her back problem. She probably has more PTSD than me. She doesn't sleep much." A quiver overwhelmed me. "The fact that I saw a flash of my bloodied sister after her fall terrified me, only I didn't realize that until now—I was frightened. At the time, I was only the bearer of the news." I put my hand over my heart.

"You poor thing. You were a young girl too. No one comforted you. But Lily survived." My gentle therapist smiled. "I'll be happy to work with her. Let's talk about you. How do you feel about your sister coming?"

"I feel bad for her and want her to get well, but I also want to poke my eyes out." I twisted my fingers together. "Why am I stuck with these people? I attract them because I have a big house? My mother wants me to take care of everyone. There's often a hidden agenda and I am it."

"Let's do some hypnosis and lift the powerlessness you feel. What is the intention we are setting?" Barbara inched her chair toward the recliner while I pushed down its back.

"Sue wants to heal from feeling helpless so she can be free. Free from diseases and angst." I wiggled in the recliner to get comfortable.

"Beautiful." Barbara covered me with the blanket.

Through the usual relaxation procedure, I got still. I pictured myself in my usual warm, sunlit flower meadow.

"We are going to take your mind high up. Higher and higher." Barbara counted from one to ten, and asked me to go to a wise, joyous, loving place. "What do you see?"

"Birds on a mountaintop."

"Want to go higher?"

"No. This is good. My father loved birds. He used to swing them in cages during a stroll. They sang melodies. He put dark drapes around the cages to keep them calm." I adjusted my head in the recliner. "There was this black bird we had for years. Had a white beak and wasn't a songbird. My mother taught it to say good morning in Taiwanese. '*Gao-tza!*' It said this whenever you walked by. Even at nighttime. It was a feisty bird that pecked people."

Barbara sipped her water.

"One day I came home from school and found the bird lying at the bottom of the cage, eyes closed. Its chest puffed slightly in and out. Its beak dropped open." I stirred under the blanket. "My mother said, 'Your father feed bird. It bite. He grab bird, throw on ground. I put back in cage, say *gao-tza*, it no speak. Poor bird.' My mother's nose was pink. She had cried. The bird died a few hours later. My father's cruelty scared me." Eyes shut, I wiped my face and blew my nose.

A black-and-white picture that captured Lily's howling face floated to my head. Standing next to me, her mouth was in the shape of an upside-down U.

"And in another family photo. Ba slapped Lily and I couldn't help her." I shivered. "It was sudden and she wailed. I don't know ... my heart literally hurts now. I hate that man, the man who wanted to be revered as a father. What kind of a father hits kids and kills pets? And I know we've talked about my mother, the sacrificial victim. I am sick of her too. She helps me and now I have to cough up something for her."

"Sue, I am sorry for what happened. Is there anything you want to say to your parents?"

The knowledge of me as an infant came in. I was on a hard wooden platform bed, feeling afraid. The screaming in the room felt unsafe. Ma, my caretaker, was upset. "I know they're fighting. My mother's getting hit and she doesn't back down. Stop, you guys!" Heart racing, I breathed hard and paused a long few minutes. Even under relaxation, I made fists under the blanket. "That's it. I'm finished with this household," I declared.

Eyes closed, I turned my head toward Barbara. "I see the adult Sue taking the infant me from the bed. And the adult me tells my parents, you had your chance. I am taking this child with me and I will take care of her. We are done here."

"Good for you!" Barbara's voice was a pitch higher than usual.

"I'm not responsible for any of your suffering. You chose to have kids. I'm not going to feel guilty for being your burden anymore. I'm done paying my debt to you. I'm going to take care of myself, since you didn't ..." I swallowed. "Or couldn't. Sorry you lived through World War II and were treated like shit as children. I'm done waiting for you to be nice to me! I'm done being a victim, being stuck with you."

"Wow," Barbara cheered.

"I see the back of adult Sue holding the infant Shogi and walking out of the room."

The past is not the present, but it informs it. I was changing the past.

"How does the baby Sue look?" Barbara asked.

"She looks relieved, like her hell is over. Her life isn't in peril or in someone else's hands anymore." I grinned.

"How interesting. The adult self will watch out for her."

"Can you tell her that the adult you will never, ever leave her? That you will always take care of her." Barbara stopped and inhaled. "And tell her she doesn't have to be perfect to be alive."

I took a few minutes to "look" at my baby self, slanted-eyes with pursed lips under a small flat nose, wrapped in a thick brown blanket. I mentally told the baby that I would be with her forever, and that she could do whatever she liked. "Little Sue is happy. She laughed."

"Great. Tell her that her mother survived and you grew up to help save her. Everything is okay."

The brilliance of Barbara. She tied up the loose ends. "Have your adult self assure the infant you, the six-year-old you, the thirteen year-old ... all the way until now, that the adult Sue will be there for all of them. You can hug them all if you wish."

That took a while. I saw my selves in a visual timeline. I hugged every one of them and said, I love you, I will not leave you. I collected pieces of my being that were trapped in time. It was like meeting an old friend who understood me all along. How strange and wonderful.

"As a creative measure, I melted all the me's inside my heart. We're together now." I said.

"Excellent! Good for you."

A few minutes passed. "Thank you, Barbara. Am I all healed?"

"Ask," she said, as she often did. It instilled in me that the answer was within.

"Not sure ..."

"That's okay. You did a lot today. Do you feel your power now?"

"Every ounce of me. Ha!" An image of me lying on a scale at a deli counter came to mind.

I came out of the trance and opened my puffy eyes. It was like taking a vivid nap. "That was huge. Thank you so much. We went way over again," I said.

"It worked out that way."

"Since I am a visual person, my gratitude for you is erupting from a volcano this minute."

Barbara gave me hug. Somehow her tall stature made it even better. She was the compassionate witness I needed. I left therapy loving the cool air in the dusk and the chirping birds in the trees. Birds held significance for me since childhood. They represented freedom and divine chatter. I sent a silent hello to the birds in my life, the black one in childhood, and Jonah, which meant "dove" in Hebrew. I equated white birds with his spirit.

I felt transformed. I would face the trial of Lily's stay with a whole self instead of a fractured one. I wondered how the mind's triumph would manifest in the external world.

CHAPTER TWENTY-NINE

"Sue-Yi, people should hire you to smell their houses," my sister said. Her taunting eyes perched above her cheekbones. Lips parted slightly, her smirk invited challenge. Everything about Lily was round. Face, hips, calves. She stood by the kitchen counter, bare toes splayed on the floor.

"I am trying to keep the house chemical free. I asked you and mother what that weird smell was." On one occasion I found Ma using bleach in her bathroom.

"You seem very sensitive about smells, that's all." Lily spun away from me and headed for the stairs.

"That's right. I am." I went after her but stopped after two steps. "I take care of my life to stay healthy," I called out, refraining from saying more because our mother was nearby and I was allegedly over helplessness. I sat down and stared at the walls, pondering what my adult–inner child pair could do about my sister.

Lily probably did not believe chemical sensitivity was real. She only saw me setting rules, eating clean, jogging, and driving to work or to see Barbara. She did not see my face when the condition was dire. Her one-month stay had surpassed five months, with no end in sight. I gazed at my mother, who was busy feeding plates to the dishwasher.

To what extent should I take care of Lily, Ma?

My mother slammed shut the dishwasher and caught my frown. She went for the stairway as if she had something pressing to do. I felt like Ba—we used to vacate the room the second the air around him changed.

Lily saw Barbara once and sent a thanks-but-no-thanks note. I offered to find another therapist but she declined. I could not convince my sister that reconciling her inner demons, in addition to medical interventions, could rid her of her pains. Since I had found a way to heal, I thought it might be easier for her to follow suit. I was wrong. She took a few trips for job interviews, had physical therapy, and swam at the town pool. Most of the time she lay in our mother's bed watching TV with her laptop.

I walked down the hall to Roger's office and sat in the loveseat. "I can't believe she mocked me. When and how's she going to move out?" Next to me, December snow weighed on rhododendron branches outside the floor-length windows.

"Lily has choices," Roger said. Behind his black swivel chair, piles of papers fell sideways on shelves. "It's time to let her go. You can't solve the problem for her." Roger was big on being proactive, a quality that resonated. It was the opposite of how I was raised.

"Her back is better but the economy has gone to pot," I said. "Taxpayers are bailing out Wall Street. It's hard for Lily to find a job."

"You are enabling her to not deal with life," Whac-A-Mole Roger declared.

My eyes widened. I had extended Lily's stay to three months after she came down with a virus. I filled myself with patience, took walks with her, counseled, and hoped for a turning point. Support was the intention. "My sister had traumas," I reminded Roger. "Once we were walking, a squirrel in a bush made her jump. Talk about skittish. I don't know how she shot crime scenes for work before. She might be depressed too. That takes a lifetime of work." I would know.

"Even if she is, she needs to want to take care of herself. You can't do it for her. She can't check out here indefinitely. It's going on six months. She doesn't think she needs to talk to a therapist."

I rested my head on the back of the sofa and talked at the ceiling. "Lily isn't interested in healing emotional issues. She said she needs to fix her back first. I guess anxiety and muscle tension aren't related in her world."

"What are you going to do about it?" Roger said.

I had been thoughtful about Lily's needs but she remained closed off. She did not do dishes, cook, communicate whether she would eat dinner, or tell me when she finished foods in the pantry so I could replace them. Her shrill voice hung in the air when I got home from work. I clenched my jaw at night and paid a therapist to cope. The dizziness had subsided but my sense of wholeness was thinning.

In my mind I saw my adult Sue hugging baby Shogi and putting her to rest in a crib. Something ended. "Let's ask Lily what the deal is." My resistance to being the bad guy vanished. "My mother will think we are asking Lily to leave and be upset. But she's probably expecting it." Ma was no fool when it came to imposing on others. We had lived with three of her seven sisters.

"We're asking for a plan, not for Lily to leave," Roger said.

"Right. This way she can have a goal and work toward it." Why did not I think of that? As much as I battled with Roger, when there was a crisis, his cool thinking and consideration came through.

I went downstairs and asked Lily to come up. She followed me to the office. I returned to the loveseat, and Roger joined me. Lily sat in the black office chair Roger had rolled from behind the desk.

"Lily, you've been here for over five months. We're glad that your back is better." I spoke with my associate director voice. "We'd like to know what your thinking is, about your stay here."

"I don't know." Lily swiveled in the chair facing us. She pouted and her face flushed. "I mean, thanks for helping me out and letting me live here. I am having a hard time finding a job. I look online everyday ... You want me to move out?" Her eyes welled up.

"Not right away. But would you figure out what you'll do and tell us?" I approached the ticking bomb.

Roger pulled back his feet and leaned forward. "We need to know what your plan is."

"Okay. OKAY. I'll move out soon!" She burst into tears. "You ... you ... surprised me with this meeting." She rubbed one eye with curled fingers, a mannerism I knew well.

A surprise? Roger and I looked at each other.

"We didn't ask you to move out. We asked for a plan." I implored.

My sister propelled out of the rolling chair and left. It hit the wall with a thump.

~

"Mommy, is Amah going to move out?" Noah asked from the back of my car the following day.

My ears stood up. "Who told you that?"

"Umm ... Aunt Lily?"

Lily's stay was the issue, not my mother's. I had promised to have Ma at our home for life and Roger agreed to that. What were my mother and Lily plotting? Why was my ten-year-old giving me the news? I parked in our driveway, ran inside, and stormed by Ma. Lily was in bed watching TV.

"Why is Noah saying Mother might move out?" I shut the bedroom door, leaving my mother's startled face behind it.

"I'll leave in a month, January." My sister moved her eyes off of the screen. "I don't know. Mother might come with me?"

"She might? Why?"

Lily stared.

"Did you find a job?" I asked.

"Not yet."

"If you have plans, you tell me or Roger. We are the adults. Don't put Noah in the middle." I knew what that was like growing up.

"I didn't put him in the middle. I just told him like ... a friend." Lily switched off the TV.

"He is a child. Not a friend." The lack of boundaries in my family became painfully clear. "Noah is worried about Mother moving out. You know she drives him to school and back every day." I folded my trembling arms over my stomach.

"Sorry, I didn't realize." My sister began to cry.

"I'm sorry things are ending this way. I really tried to help and hope you'll find an interesting job and that your back gets even better."

We were not in the same boat anymore.

I turned to leave and opened the door to Ma's teary face. She wished to speak to me and Roger. I ran to get him. "The shit's hitting the fan." I said. "My mother is waiting for us in the TV room."

While we stood, Ma sat in a chair against the dark paneled wall. "I ... ah ... thinking about moving out."

"Why?" My brows furled. "We said you can live with us. You're living with us."

"Lily move out. I move too." She sucked in her reddened nose.

"You have to help Lily?" I demanded. It was that life-and-death attachment since Lily's childhood accident.

Ma sniffled.

After a long pause, Roger piped up. "Okay. If you want."

My silence was a tacit agreement with him. My mother got up and shuffled out of the room.

I prided myself on never going back on my words. But if my mother really wanted to leave, I could not stop her. I felt bad limiting her use of the house after telling her to treat it like home, but drew the line at accommodating another family member long term. Finally, disappointing my mother sat okay with me. I could withstand her crying and dissatisfaction. I did not need to say yes then agonize over how it would cost me.

Roger and I sat down, looking out the backyard. I said, "Is my mother really willing to give up her life here? She loves the gardening, Noah, shopping at Whole Foods, and the security of being with us. All for Lily?"

"Your mom might think we need her, and this is her way of getting us to ask her to stay, then she'll include Lily in the deal."

Maybe. Ma, who also collected rent from a property in New York, had offered to increase the fifty dollars Lily contributed monthly. I refused the money. There was no way of knowing if Lily was going to be okay when she moved out, and no way of knowing if she did not try.

"As long as my sister is single and Ma lives with us, there's a chance I get my sister too." I held Roger's hand. "That's not fair, especially to you. I have to let go. I can't protect them forever."

A spell was broken. I surrendered to the dynamic and would no longer feed it. It belonged to the past. I did not need to save others in order to save myself. By acting on their behalf, I avoided my own angst. It was the Styrofoam version of being in control. MCS showed me I could not keep up the charade. Blind selflessness was a hemorrhage of energy. It rendered me a house of cards that crumbled when life dealt its blows.

I would help from a grounded place, not a hijacked psyche. I was humbled by the difficulty that brought on this "healing crisis." Eldest sister or not, I was done with my imaginary omnipotence. It was time to let others walk their paths.

CHAPTER THIRTY

"Let's sell the house in the beginning of spring. It's a key time, right after the winter." Roger beamed over the kitchen table. Edie, our real estate broker sat beside him.

"We can do that," Edie agreed. "How about mid-March? I have a great contractor and crew that can work on weekends." Our super broker's pale blue eyes shone under her deep brow bones. Edie sold our first home at lightning speed years ago. It was a hot market then, unlike now.

Our house needed an overhaul. Stress, dust, and possibly chemicals would be in my face from this moment on. Maybe the chemical sensitivity would not be an issue.

I knew Edie would want the property to look finished, sparse, and inviting to the next homeowner. I surveyed the kitchen. The bright overhead light revealed six blotches on the ceiling and walls where Roger spackled.

We never got around to painting them because we focused on getting me well. All ten rooms in the house were like this, in a perpetual half-done state. We also had shelves of books, tools, and dishes. And furniture inherited from my father in-law's office, Roger's grandma's apartment, and our parents' homes.

"You guys," I said before sipping my tea. "It's March first. We're talking about selling in two weeks. How about three weeks? We should prep the place well."

"March twenty-first then. No later," Roger conceded. "I don't want to lose the momentum of the season." He pulled on his cap. His eagerness irritated me a bit but I understood it. "We should spend the least amount of money to sell it quickly," he added.

A gamble in a down economy. I nodded to emphasize Roger's point. After Lily moved out in January, we started to wonder why we toiled to live in an affluent suburb and a climate that was bleak almost half of the year.

We toured the house with Edie to explore the work needed. Back at the kitchen table, she rattled off projects while Roger jotted in a notebook. "... rip out the wood paneling and put in wall boards, update the master bath, paint all walls—"

"Make sure you get low-VOC paint." I put my hands around my mug. VOCs, volatile organic compounds, are toxic chemicals emitted from solid or liquid materials. "In case the house doesn't sell, we'd still need to live in it."

"I go to a store in Concord that sells no-VOC paint," Edie said with a nod.

"Even better." One weight dropped from my shoulders.

"We should skim coat the popcorn ceilings. These ceilings should be flat," Edie implored with a certainty that was not expected from her petite, soft appearance.

The weight got added back on. Skim coating? Would that involve chemicals and sanding everywhere?

"The ceiling looks clean," Roger noted. That's a big job to do nine rooms. It sounds like it would cost a lot."

I turned to Edie. "Is that really important? We don't need to have smooth ceilings ..."

"In Lexington you do." The realtor dipped her chin, imparting knowledge from being a broker here for over two decades.

Were we so classy in Lexington that only flat ceilings would do? I raised my eyebrows and opened my mouth.

"We want to get the highest dollar for this house," Edie cut in.

My mouth clammed shut. As the Great Recession kicked in, Roger's clients stopped calling. Even Wellesley College rumored layoffs. We had decided to sell at the worst possible time.

"If we do the ceiling, then we have to move out. The dust and chemicals might be a problem. That means more expenses," I said. I had explained the MCS to Edie. The fewer triggers for me, the better.

"Two weeks at a hotel," Roger wrote on his list.

I jiggled my knee under the table, a nervous habit. The dust from the construction would require a cleaning crew. That would be Roger and me, as funds would be spent on lodging. After deliberating the budget and timeline, we signed a contract with Edie and walked her out.

Standing at the entryway facing our crammed storage room, I blew up my cheeks. "Rog, this is gonna be a rollercoaster ride. I hope I can handle it."

"I hope you can too." He turned swiftly to shut the front door. In it was a viewing window with three carved rungs vertically across it. It always felt like looking out from jail.

Not for long ...

"If we don't sell it right away, we'll be twenty-five thousand dollars in the hole," Roger reminded me. "This has to work." He focused on my face.

"I agree." I sat on the lower part of the stairway, my feet on the cold slate floor. "I have to address something. My mother." After the circus over Lily, Ma did not move out. My sister said she could not handle our mother's fretting but left with Ma's older car.

"You better let her know what's happening. I gotta start fixing this place." Roger ran up the steps.

My mother had repeatedly talked about living in her New York property before selling it. It was her tax planning. I dismissed the idea of her moving back but she said she didn't know the future, not wanting to commit to our place or hers. Two days ago we told her our decision to move, possibly to a sunnier state. Her eyes popped open. She thought we would never leave Massachusetts because Roger had family in the area.

I poked my head into Ma's bedroom. "We have one week to pack and move out before renovation." I explained the list of projects. "We should store or get rid of anything we don't need because the house should look fairly empty when we show it."

"You fix my room? I move right away?"

"No. Edie said it's okay. It just needs to be neat."

"I go New York to my rental this weekend. Store things." Her tenants' lease ended in July. She needed housing for four months. "I find a room for next month?"

"Yes—in case this place is sold quickly. Sorry for the short notice, Ma."

In the dim of her lamp, in front of a wall where she tacked up Noah's artwork, I gazed at my mother with a rock in my stomach. I had invited her to live with us. This was her home. "Please tell me if you need help packing."

She looked down to her beige slippers and back up to me. "*Herh.*"

~

Once Edie was engaged to work with us, my urge to purge woke from years of stupor. We made carloads to Goodwill. I hopped on the Internet and merrily gave away treasures on Craigslist—a drum set, college chairs, a futon, children's bikes, crystal bowls, scuba tank, the Mosquito Magnet, bookcases ... I loved that our life was getting lighter, and the receivers of these items left with glee.

The night before the workers came, Roger and I were up till three o'clock covering furniture, labeling and moving boxes to the attic. To keep things from aggravating the MCS or allergies, Roger wrapped our bedding inside thick, black trash bags and I sealed them with heavy-duty tape. I was touched by his thoroughness about my needs during the frenzy. I stuffed the Volvo with suitcases and bags packed to get us through the next two weeks, and joined Ma and Noah at a nearby inn. I did not tell anyone at work that we were selling our place, fearing I would be on the chopping block during a layoff. I would go to work as usual and keep things constant while we went through the upheaval at home.

~

A few days into the renovation, I drove to the house. Two white trucks were parked along its front, and morning birds chirped. The sun sparkled behind our raised ranch. I squinted and traced its linear, long outline. We had moved here from a suffocating place where we lost Jonah. My idyllic notion of a permanent home did not pan out.

A worker on a ladder swiped strokes of paint on the trim of the two-car garage. I waved good morning to the master contractor. He smiled back. From my bag I retrieved a blue face mask, and pulled its elastic over my head. It snapped tight, startling me.

Inside the house, a sour smell hung in the air. My senses lit up like a fire alarm. *What is that? Where is it coming from?* I squeezed the mask against my nose to ensure a tight seal. Dust and debris from scraped popcorn ceilings covered every surface, giving the whole place a white, ghostly sheen. My feet crunched on plastic sheets that lined the wood floor. In the kitchen, I ran my fingers over cobalt-blue painter's tape that Ma and I had applied over the seams of the cabinets. I knew that fine dust from sanding got past barriers, despite the tape. I sighed. Cleanup would be a load of fun.

Twap-twap. Twap-twap. The sound led me to my study at the other end of the house. A man in a faded baseball cap and paint-splattered jeans stood near the top of a ladder. He wielded a large putty knife over his head and spread a white goop with it. The source of the smell.

"What are you putting on the ceiling?" My muffled voice came under my mask.

"Excuse me, ma'am?" He looked down.

I asked again, lifting my mask a little. Edie knew about the MCS and promised to use nontoxic materials. Surely she communicated that to her team?

"Plaster." He glanced at me and went back to smoothing the ceiling.

"Plaster? Thanks." I recognized the stench from Roger's home-improvement projects.

Plaster is nontoxic? Yes. Get a grip.

I checked and double-checked with myself. No dizziness, nausea, brain fog. Given the anxiety and lack of sleep so far, I was doing well. I turned and left the study with a grin under the mask.

In the backyard, I found my mother raking leaves and walked over to her.

"Ma, thanks for helping with Noah and the house. I'm sorry that your things were packed badly last week." Seeing her upended and still assisting, my eyes welled up.

My mother had returned from Long Island to find her life being boxed up by Edie's associate and me. While she was away, we decided to redo her room after all. "No-no-no," my mother protested, shaking her head. "I no know what clothes to pack. Now between seasons!" She emptied the boxes. She would do it herself. I backed away, trying to contain my guilt about her loss of dignity.

Ma's headful of gray bopped as she clawed at the dirt. I patted her back. "Really, Ma. *Sieh-sieh.*"

"*Meh-la, meh-la.* (It's nothing.) We help each other." She kept her eyes on the brown lawn beneath us. "Best place I live. Here. Beautiful yard. Trees, big rocks."

It was gorgeous partly because my mother spent every spring and summer weeding among a huge patch of prickly junipers. We did not use pesticides. For hours Ma stooped under a white sun hat and dug into the earth with a small spade. If my to-do list wasn't so humungous, I might have appreciated what it all meant in that moment.

The day before the open house, Roger and I cleared away more yard waste. He laid stone steps in a rock garden. I found someone to haul away cinder blocks and extra tools. Ma and I washed the dusty floors and surfaces repeatedly with nontoxic cleaners. It might have been faster to use conventional cleaning products, but I thought it was better to stay natural.

Inside, painters accentuated the walls with muted green and yellow. Our home had transformed into an elegant residence. It already felt like someone else's. Night came without notice. Ma left to tend to Noah, who was watching marathon TV at the inn.

In the storage room, Roger pointed to the areas vacated by bookcases and files cabinets. "It needs bleach. It's grounded-in grime," he said.

"Bleach?" I raised my voice. "Clorox?" I had done so well so far. Did I want to expose myself to chemicals?

"Yes, Sue. It's half past midnight. The open house is tomorrow. I have been working nonstop for three weeks. I'm tired." Roger walked around the room defined by dirty beige linoleum. "We've never washed this room. It was not clean to begin with," he said.

"A fresh house shows better. Could we try the nontoxic spray first?" I grabbed the sponge mop and bucket at the far end of the room. "Come on." My arms felt like lead. The mop felt like lead.

Roger filled the bucket with water while I sprayed citrus cleaner at a six-by-twelve-inch stain and dropped to my knees with a scrub brush. The suds went from white to light gray. After mopping it, most of the mark remained.

"Shit." I shook the water from the brush and went at it again. I really did not want to break out the Clorox.

"It's not doing much." Roger pushed on the sponge mop and rubbed.

"Fuck it. Go for the bleach," I finally dared.

"Here it goes." He unscrewed the top of the Clorox as I backed away three feet. He mixed it with the water in the bucket.

Bleh. Bleach. The pungent odor permeated the room, zinging my nose. It was like reuniting with an old friend who fell out of favor. My husband soaked the mop in the bucket and went at one stain. I stepped toward him and stared at the floor. The dark spot vanished in seconds. The marvel of chemicals.

"Ooh. It's good!" I pointed at the bucket.

"How are you doing?" Roger looked up at me.

Let's see ...

Head: check.

Balance: check.

Stomach: check.

Inner child: check. This is fun trying the bleach.

Adult Sue-Yi: check. She definitely wants to show a clean house.

"All right, Rog—I am okay! Let's finish so we can go to bed." I laughed. "Wahoo!"

We scoured and wiped, bleach and all, and locked up.

"Pretty good, Sue-Yi!" Roger exclaimed in the car.

"If I can handle Clorox in a closed room, I am done with the chemical sensitivity." It did not matter that it was three in the morning. I declared myself a healed woman.

CHAPTER THIRTY-ONE

We drove by the open house on reconnaissance. "There're many cars here," Roger said, pointing. "Hope that means lots of buyers." I counted cars on the street. Fifteen.

Edie held showings on the weekend, yielding over sixty potential buyers. She informed them that we would hear offers the following Monday. Our bold tactic to sell in such a market worked. The house attracted six bids. We would all move out soon.

It was two days after our wedding anniversary, the first day of spring. We had bought the home exactly eight years ago. It held my dreams and nightmares, my family and its dysfunctions, our energies and affection for each other. It was also where I uncovered and exorcised my demons. I thanked the house and blessed it for the young family who would live there.

~

Two weeks later, a van full of my mother's things waited on our slanted driveway. Roger would drive it behind Ma's car to New York.

Standing in the front yard, I said to my mother, "I appreciate everything you've done for us, Ma. Sorry this was so unexpected." I repeated the sentiment.

"It's okay. Take care yourself and family. Be safe." My mother smiled. Behind her, yellow daffodils swayed in the sun. "*Sieh-sieh-la.* You take care of me too." She turned to face the front door. "Beautiful house."

"You helped to make it lovely, Ma."

"Noah, be good. Listen to Mommy, Daddy." My mother turned to our son and he nodded, resting his large brown eyes on her wrinkled face. "Come to New York visit me." She smoothed his hair and hugged him.

With wet eyes, I followed my mother to her sedan, its backseat filled with boxes and plants. Ma had a green thumb. She bought wilted African violets on sale and nursed them into vibrant, gorgeous plants.

"Drive carefully," I said, leaning in the driver's window. The new car smell, an issue for MCS sufferers, didn't bother me.

"*Herh. Herh.* Take care." Ma waved and turned the car around at the cul-de-sac. The gravel beneath her crunched. We waved back and Roger followed with the van. Both vehicles disappeared down the street. I exhaled deeply as Noah ran in the house. I cautioned him to keep it neat—it was still staged for the buyer.

Sitting on the front step, I wept. We could not have accomplished this feat without my mother. She never complained about being thrown into a sudden move after living with us for over six years. I helped free her from her marriage and she rallied to get me out of this house. We liberated each other, a soul contract fulfilled. Ma gave the unconditional love I sought many times. In this move, there was no judgment, strings attached, or drama. I saw my mother in her best intentions.

I was well. My own person. There was a new home within me. I loved that I could pause and ask my inner child if she was happy, sad, or wanted a treat. Despite the ill will I put on my body, it remained intact, open to thrive.

Is this for real, Jonah? Give me a sign.

I gazed at the cloudless, blue sky.

A seagull shot over the aspen next to me. The white bird circled over the house, gliding effortlessly.

Indeed. I am free.

ACKNOWLEDGEMENTS

To Roger, who prevailed during the difficult times and endured the process of birthing this book, your love sustains and inspires me. And to Noah, whose uniqueness, brilliance, and childhood gave me reasons to keep going every day for the last eighteen years. I love you.

Gratitude to Ba, Ma, and *mei-mei*, I have learned many soul lessons from sharing our lives. I hold you in light.

Barbara M. Johnson, I am awed by your intuition and compassion. You are my teacher for life.

A big thanks to Molly Runcie and Gail Storey, my Most Tireless Readers, and to Lori Carter, Deidre Lin, Lotus Kemna, Tinling Choong, and Sandra Mayo, for your time and discerning comments.

Thank you, Jody Berman, for your eagle eye and insightful, detailed editing.

My heart as a mother is shared by Sarina Baptista and Pamela Daniels—our bond is forever.

A bow to Katie Gallanti, for your care and superb guidance.

Amy Kiffe, Bonnie Collins, Diane Lisowski, and Norah Wakula: Your cheerleading buoyed me during this long journey. I hope to read your memoirs soon.

Deep appreciation to my writing teachers: Lisa Jones, whose class manifested the prologue, and Sibyl Johnston, who initiated me into memoir writing.

Thank you, Judy Tsafrir, Paula Youmell, Jasmin Lee Cori, Amy Law, and Karen Shih, for your generosity and resonance.

Kristin Long—your sharp mind and enthusiasm made the finishing line glow like sunshine.

ABOUT THE AUTHOR

 Sue Wang is a Reiki Master Teacher and psychological astrologer who found her calling after healing from a life-changing loss and an unexplained illness. As an energy intuitive, Sue helps fellow seekers reclaim the essence and power within via the mind-body-spirit connection. She writes for online publications to promote energy healing and peaceful, harmonious living. Sue is a graduate of Wellesley College and the Harvard Graduate School of Education, and worked as a career counselor and administrator until moving from Massachusetts to Boulder, Colorado in 2009. Visit her at www.Connect2Self.com.